D1511315

The Urbana Free Library

To renew materials call
217-367-4057

MODERN
NATIONS
—OF THE—
WORLD

FRANCE

TITLES IN THE MODERN NATIONS OF THE WORLD SERIES INCLUDE:

Austria
Brazil
Canada
China
Cuba
England
Ethiopia
Germany
Greece
Haiti
India
Italy
Japan
Jordan
Kenya
Mexico
Norway
Russia
Saudi Arabia
Scotland
Somalia
South Africa
South Korea
Sweden
Switzerland
Taiwan
United States

FRANCE

BY LAUREL CORONA

LUCENT BOOKS
SAN DIEGO, CALIFORNIA

THOMSON

GALE

*Detroit • New York • San Diego • San Francisco
Boston • New Haven, Conn. • Waterville, Maine
London • Munich*

1-03   27.45

To the Estevez-Barros and Cortese families, and especially to Lucie.
De tout mon coeur, je vous remercie.

Library of Congress Cataloging-in-Publication Data

Corona, Laurel, 1949–
    France / by Laurel Corona.
        p.   cm. — (Modern nations of the world)
    Includes bibliographical references and index.
    Summary: Examines the history of France from prehistoric times to
the twentieth century and discusses its culture, daily life, economics, and
social changes.
    ISBN 1-56006-760-8 (hard : alk. paper)
    1. France—Juvenile literature. [1. France.] I. Title.   II. Series.
DC17 .C68 2002
944—dc21
                                                                            2001005478

Copyright © 2002 by Lucent Books,
an imprint of The Gale Group,
10911 Technology Place, San Diego, CA 92127
Printed in the U.S.A.

CONTENTS

INTRODUCTION

THE MANY SIDES OF FRANCE

The casual map reader, if asked to describe the shape of France, might reply that it resembles a star. The French, however, have nicknamed their country "the hexagon." This nickname has stuck because it says something important about the way the French view France. From the time of the ancient Arab and Greek mathematicians, geometric shapes have suggested that a divine order exists in the world. Though the French are noted for their willingness to criticize their country and fellow citizens, nevertheless most feel that being French is special and that living in France is better than liv-

ing anywhere else. Being born inside the hexagon—or put another way, being unfortunate enough to be born outside it—contributes to a strong sense of national identity despite the tremendous geographic and social diversity of the country and its long history of internal divisiveness.

DIVISIVENESS AND UNITY

This simultaneous unity and divisiveness is illustrated by what the Paris newspapers called in the mid-1980s "The Battle of the Belfry Towers." Three towns near Bourges, in the Berry region, each claimed to be the exact geographic center of France. The towns were quite different from each other physically and politically. Two were very poor: One was a dusty truck stop, while another was, according to former *New York Times* Paris Bureau Chief Richard Bernstein, "a genuinely rural hamlet . . . , little more than a row of two-story stone houses decorated with painted wood shutters and surrounded by agricultural fields." The third was "affluent and well groomed,"[1] filled with brightly colored flower beds and window boxes. Each town had built a monument on what it claimed was the exact center of France, to promote itself as a place for tourists to stop for a photograph, thus boosting the town's economy if the tourists also bought food or souvenirs.

These villages are located in what is called "La France Profonde" ("Deep France"), a term used for rural France, which is generally agricultural, usually poor, and characterized by small towns and villages. Contrasted with Deep France is urban France. Residents of Paris, the capital city, are immensely amused by the Battle of the Belfry Towers because it is so obvious to them that physical geography has nothing to do with the matter. The true center of France is Paris itself. The proudest among the French would claim that Paris is the center of Europe and even in some respects the center of the world. What stories such as the Battle of the Belfry Towers illustrate, however, is the country's essential unity. After all, if being one country were not important, finding the geographic center—or even looking down one's nose at those trying to do it—would never have become an issue.

A COUNTRY WITHOUT COMPARISON

France is a country in which everything abounds, so the French seem justified in their pride in being inside the hexagon, regardless of where they live. Their history includes many of the greatest figures and most stirring cultural, social, and political events in human history. Today France is renowned worldwide for food, fashion, and art. In many circles, to say something is French is to imply that it is unsurpassed in quality and inventiveness.

Paris is indisputably the main symbol of France and the heart of French culture, history, and contemporary life, but it is only outside of Paris that one can begin to appreciate the true abundance and diversity of this land. Its scenery rivals any in the world, from the French Alps to the rugged Brittany coast, from the forests of the Dordogne to the wheat fields of the Midi, from the vineyards of the Loire Valley to the sunny Riviera. Its geography lends itself to the production of an extraordinary range of products, from its world-famous wines and cheeses, to sunflowers, oysters, mineral water, and air-dried salt. Its industries produce a wide range of products, from cookware and textiles to cars.

One of the most visited cities in the world, Paris is renowned for its historical and cultural importance.

France also abounds in regional cultures. In parts of France it is still possible to hear people speaking regional dialects hardly recognizable as French, observe them doing their daily work much in the same way their ancestors did, and see them dressed in traditional clothing on festival days. Though small regional movements, particularly in Brittany, sometimes argue for independence from France, their efforts are not a real challenge to the unity of the nation. In fact, many French are very supportive of efforts to strengthen regional cultures. For example, recently one state university in Brittany began offering degrees in the history and culture of Brittany with courses conducted entirely in Breton, the local language. Clearly this is a sign of confidence that regional differences are not a threat but instead are one of France's many charms.

FADED GLORY, FADED FUTURE?

It is no wonder that the French are fiercely proud of their country, a pride that sometimes comes across as cultural snobbery to outsiders. However, the French today are troubled over many issues that threaten to diminish the quality of their lives and the uniqueness of their culture. Although arguably, no single country has had more impact on the history and culture of the Western world, the French have had difficulty accepting that this legacy is not enough to keep them in the forefront today. France is the largest country in Western Europe, but a medium-sized country by world standards. It is not extraordinarily endowed with valuable natural resources. Its manufacturing base is not particularly strong, and its agricultural economy, still based mostly on individual farms, is suffering from downturns because of competition from huge multinational corporations.

The adoption of a single currency (the Euro) and other changes brought about by their membership in the European Union have also caused many French people to worry that their unique identity will be lost. Close to half speak no other language, despite the country's borders with Italy,

Brittany, the peninsular region of northwest France, boasts a beautiful, rugged coastline.

Spain, and Germany, in part because they are comfortable living their lives entirely inside the hexagon. Many, even among the well educated, resist learning English precisely because they fear it will lead to the Americanization of their culture. They worry because they know they have a lot to lose. Social issues such as immigration, and political concerns such as the growth in popularity of extremist political parties on both the Left and Right, also cause many to question whether France can maintain a sense of national identity in the future.

THE ESSENTIAL FRANCE

It is common in France to hear heated discussions about where the country is headed politically, economically, socially, and culturally. It is also common for the French to fear their children will inherit a country diminished in some ways from what it has been, just as they feel they inherited a rather faded version of France themselves. Yet even the most heated discussion over the dinner table is likely to end when the food is served, because the French know how to stop and enjoy the present.

In *The Baker's Wife*, a film by the great French director Marcel Pagnol, a small-town baker stops making bread because his young wife has run away. The townspeople all band together in an effort to find the wife, because they cannot live without the wonderful bread. As long as the French put such effort into maintaining and protecting their quality of life, it seems unlikely that what makes this nation special could ever be lost. The French have an expression, "Plus ça change, plus c'est la même chose," or "The more things change, the more they stay the same." Things change, sometimes in worrisome ways, but there seems little doubt there will always be a France.

Land of Abundance

1

Writer Fernand Braudel once commented that "France is diversity."[2] Nowhere is this more apparent than in its geography. France is sometimes called Europe "in miniature" because the full range of terrains and climates of the continent are found somewhere within its borders. However, the beautiful array of rivers, mountains, rolling hills, flat pasturelands, and farms are only part of the visual picture of France. It must also include the many towns and cities, ranging from picturesque villages to one of the great capital cities of the world. And, as a final element of the picture, France contains innumerable historical sites, ranging from caves containing prehistoric drawings, to immense country palaces, to Roman ruins. France does indeed have a diversity rivaling that found anywhere on earth.

Paris and the Île-de-France

Paris is the undisputed heart of France, and one of the most beautiful and interesting cities in the world. Armed with tickets for the Paris subway, or métro, one can spend a day (or a lifetime) visiting sights ranging from ancient Roman baths to the ultramodern Pompidou Center, or simply relax in one of the city's many parks and squares. Even in the oldest parts of the city, however, a vibrant present is part of the scene. For example, the cool, serene Cluny Museum, which showcases medieval art amid Roman ruins, opens onto the Boulevard St.-Michel, known locally as the Boul' Mich', in the lively student quarter. And in the courtyard of the former royal palace, the Louvre, there is a glass pyramid, designed by Chinese American architect I.M. Pei, which in 1989 began to serve as a new entrance to the museum.

Perhaps the most famous city stroll in the world begins at the Eiffel Tower, built in 1899, then continues along the Champs-Élysées to the Arc de Triomphe, a Roman-style arch built in 1836 to commemorate the victories of one of France's great heroes, Napoléon Bonaparte. Continuing toward the center of the city, the stroller will arrive at the Place de la Concorde, highlighted by the famed Obelisk, a five-thousand-year-old monument formerly part of the tomb of Egyptian pharaoh Ramses II, and the site of the beheading of King Louis XVI in 1793. Eventually the walker will arrive at the Tuileries Gardens, once the grounds of the king's residence. At the far end of the gardens is the famed art museum, the Louvre, home to Leonardo da Vinci's painting the *Mona Lisa*, and the famed ancient Greek sculpture, the *Venus de Milo*.

At the Louvre, the walker will see the Seine, the river flowing through Paris, and can follow its banks to the beautiful Hôtel de Ville, the former city hall, and the Conciergerie, the former medieval prison where, in later centuries, many figures associated with the French Revolution were tried and condemned to death. Eventually, the route along the Seine leads to perhaps the most famous Parisian landmark of all, the cathedral of Notre-Dame de Paris, situated on a small island.

Other famous sites include the Opera Garnier, legendary home to the famous phantom; Montmartre, gathering place of famous artists and the location of the Sacré-Coeur, a beautiful white church on a hill overlooking the city. To the east lies the famous Père Lachaise Cemetery, site of the tombs of French artists such as painter Théodore Géricault and singer Edith Piaf, as well as the final resting place for many famous foreigners such as Polish composer Frédéric Chopin, British writer Oscar Wilde, and American rock star Jim Morrison.

American architect I.M. Pei's modern glass pyramid serves as an entrance to the historical Louvre museum.

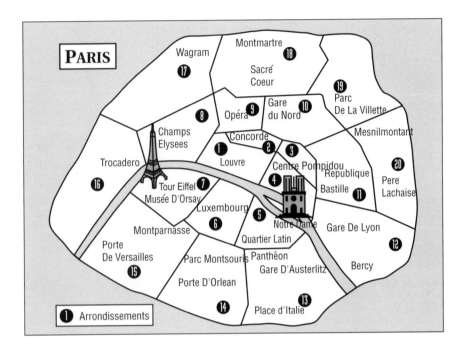

Such sights are part of the heritage of France, but they are only the most obvious evidence of the cultural richness of this amazing city. For many, the best symbol of Paris is the sidewalk café, where people enjoy espresso while reading the paper, debating the issues of the day, or people watching. For others, Paris is best symbolized by the boutiques and fashion houses, or perhaps the numerous luxury hotels and restaurants in the city. But many believe one must get away from the center into the outlying arrondissements, or districts, to see the true Paris, to witness the human diversity and energy of the city.

The region surrounding Paris is called the Île-de-France. Many homes of the famous have been turned into museums in this area, including Giverny, the beautiful garden retreat of painter Claude Monet. Famous châteaus (country palaces) abound, including Fontainebleau, the former residence of Napoléon. However, by far the most famous sight in the Île-de-France is Louis XIV's immense and lavish seventeenth-century palace at Versailles.

THE WEST COAST
Along the northern border with Belgium the region known as Picardy, with its rich soil and gentle river valleys, is excellent

The palace at Versailles, Louis XIV's home during the seventeenth century, is a popular tourist attraction.

for agriculture. Similar terrain extends through Belgium into the Netherlands, creating a route for invaders throughout the centuries and giving the area a particularly bloody history. Farther inland the soil is chalky, but intelligent agricultural practices over the centuries have made it yield such world-famous products as the sparkling wines that bear the name of its region, Champagne.

Northern France is also an industrial region, home to mining and factories, particularly in the area around Lille, but the scenery changes as one moves southwest into Normandy. The typical Norman landscape includes pastures with grazing cows and groves of apple trees. Charming small villages and shady country roads complete the picture of this beautiful region. Norman cider, butter, and cheese are world renowned for their quality. Normandy is also home to the famous cathedral at Rouen, site of the death of Joan of Arc, and the spectacular mountaintop abbey at Mont-Saint-Michel, near the border with Brittany.

South of Normandy the coast extends westward into the region known as Brittany. The coastal landscape here is different from anywhere else in France, consisting of colorful, surf-battered rocky cliffs, offshore reefs and islands, and natural harbors. Much of France's fishing fleet operates from ports such as Saint-Malo and picturesque small fishing villages such as Cancale, famous for oysters. The region also abounds in fashionable beach resorts such as Dinard and La Baule. Inland the terrain is rugged, characterized by "melancholy heaths"[3] covered with flowering shrubs, forested hills, and river valleys.

Southern Brittany is renowned for its prehistoric stone monuments known as menhirs, the most extensive of which are at Carnac. The ancient feel of the region is echoed in the independent spirit of the Breton people, many of whom still speak their ancestral language and wear ethnic dress at their important religious festivals, known as *pardons*. The Breton people are known for their independence, a characteristic dating from the period when the region was part of England, from which the name Brittany is derived.

Farther south lies the important port of La Rochelle and the province known by the name of its major city, Bordeaux. This area is one of the most geographically diverse in France, including huge coastal sand dunes and the marshes of Gironde and Landes. Farther inland lie the forests and woodlands of the famed Dordogne and Périgord regions. These areas, where cognac and the goose liver creation known as pâté

THE MYSTERY STONES OF FRANCE

All over France, ancestors have left behind intriguing monuments, from the Lascaux cave paintings to the rock constructions of Brittany and elsewhere. Most of these constructions consist of menhirs (single vertical stones) and dolmens (two vertical stones topped by a lintel, or cross stone). The root of these words is the same: the early Breton word "men" means stone, and thus dolmen is a table stone and menhir is a long stone. The most famous Neolithic site in France is at Carnac, in Brittany, where three groups of menhirs are arranged in ten to thirteen rows—nearly three thousand stones total, apparently having some unknown connection with nearby burial chambers. A particularly intriguing kind of menhir is found in Corsica (where more than a third of the total menhirs on French territory are found). These rocks are topped by carved faces, some wearing war gear such as helmets and daggers.

Dolmens can be found in fields all over France. Signposts point the way for the curious traveler, who may be rewarded after a trek across a field by the chance to touch and walk around a prehistoric rock construction in complete solitude, without souvenir stands or admission booths. Many of these dolmens are small and solitary and rather roughly constructed, giving little insight into their meaning, which includes their possible use in timekeeping, astronomy, or religious rituals. It is unlikely we will ever know for certain what drove our ancestors to struggle to put these heavy stones in place without any of the machinery we have today.

de foie gras are produced, are a gourmet's paradise. They are also the home of the famed Lascaux caves, where paintings from the Cro-Magnon era were discovered in 1940.

THE SPANISH BORDER

Farther south lies the border with Spain. From the coast, near the resort town of Biarritz, the border cuts across the Pyrenees, through the territory known as the Pays Basque. The Pyrenees are a rugged mountain range cut by steep, jagged gorges, which are difficult to cross. For centuries this geographic feature kept people of the region isolated and culturally distinct from both Spain and France. Several unique languages such as Catalan are proudly spoken here, and assimilation into mainstream French or Spanish culture has been deliberately resisted.

Despite their relative inaccessibility, the Pyrenees draw many outsiders. Skiing is excellent, and thermal spas attract thousands of visitors looking for cures for their ailments or just a few days of self-indulgence. Hikers can cross the Pyrenees from coast to coast on the GR 10 trail, and other roads and highways accommodate bicyclers and those traveling by car. At the eastern edge of the Pyrenees lies the city of Lourdes, one of the most famous Catholic pilgrimage sites in the world. Nearby, and far less well known, is a somber pilgrimage site of a different sort, the mountain fortress of

Prehistoric drawings cover the walls of the Lascaux caves in France's Dordogne region.

THE CANAL DU MIDI

From Roman times, rulers and merchants dreamed of building a canal to link the Atlantic coast of France with the Mediterranean coast. Sailing around Spain and through the Straits of Gibraltar not only took time but also was potentially hazardous because France and Spain were often at war. A canal would enable goods and those transporting them to stay safely in French territory for the entire journey. However, the engineering problems associated with scaling the 636-foot-high pass in the middle of the preferred shortest route proved insurmountable until the 1600s, when Pierre Paul Riquet was able to secure permission to build the 149-mile channel and the 103 locks it required. Riquet had to use his own money for the project and was eventually bankrupted by it, dying shortly before its successful completion in 1680. The canal became obsolete in the nineteenth century with the development of railroads, but in recent years it has undergone a rebirth, not for transportation of goods but of vacationers, both French and foreign, who rent holiday barges and spend leisurely days drifting along the canal, enjoying stops at the charming villages along its length.

Montségur, where in the thirteenth century two hundred Christian men, women, and children considered to be heretics were burned to death in a single mass fire. Today all that remains are the ruins of their cliff-top fortress.

At their eastern end, the Pyrenees drop off suddenly into the flat southwest corner of France. This province, known as Roussillon, is home to the major city of Toulouse and to Carcassonne, one of the best-preserved walled cities of the medieval era. Roussillon was once part of Spain, and the region maintains a strong blend of Spanish and French architectural styles and customs, noticeable in the red tiled roofs of Toulouse and the charming cathedral town of Albi.

THE SOUTH OF FRANCE

The south coast of France looks out onto the Mediterranean Sea. A generally calm and fairly warm body of water, the Mediterranean creates a mild and sunny coastal climate unlike that found anywhere else in France. In the southwest, as far as Marseille and nearby Toulon, the coastal land is flat and barely above sea level. East of Toulon, mountains rise sharply from the ocean as a backdrop for the narrow beaches of the famed French Riviera. The flat terrain around Avignon and Montpellier is the result of eons of erosion from the surrounding mountains down the Rhône River, which has its source several hundred miles away in the Alps.

Southwestern coastal France is a fertile plain, home to important old Roman settlements at Nîmes and Arles, as well as the location of several important larger cities—Montpellier (home to one of Europe's major universities) and Avignon, seat of the brief Avignon papacy in the fourteenth century. This region also is the site of the famous Camargue, a land of tidal estuaries and sloughs, and the site of the medieval walled city of Aigues-Mortes, from which the First Crusade was launched in 1095. This part of France was formerly called Oc, and its present name, Languedoc, refers to the ancient language of the inhabitants.

Roughly midway across the Mediterranean coast of France lies Marseille, one of the country's most important port cities. Marseille is the gateway to Provence, renowned for its fields of lavender (used for making perfumes) and sunflowers, made famous by Dutch painter Vincent van Gogh, who spent the last years of his troubled life in the area. A few miles east of Marseille the beautiful mountains known as the Alpes de Provence and the Alpes Maritimes begin their rise, dotted by spectacular little towns perched on rocky cliffs overlooking the Mediterranean. Approaching the Italian border, east of the fabled resort city of Cannes, with its world-famous film festival, and the graceful sun-drenched city of Nice, is the principality of Monaco, an independent nation of only a few square miles, and site of the famous casino at Monte Carlo.

THE FRENCH ALPS

Along the Italian border are mountains of increasing elevation, stretching north to the slopes of Mont Blanc, the highest mountain in Europe, which looks out over Italy, Switzerland, and France. The Alps are characterized by rugged, rocky peaks, snow-topped year-round; breathtaking valleys dotted with farming villages; torrential rivers and waterfalls; and lazy meadow streams. The best-known towns in the French Alps are ski resorts such as Chamonix,

but the region is also home to many charming towns such as Evian, famed for its water.

EASTERN FRANCE

The western slopes of the Alps drop quickly onto the great Rhône River plain. Here, where the Saône and the Rhône Rivers meet, lies Lyon, the "second city" of France, so called because of its importance as a cultural, industrial, and commercial center. Looming over the town is Fourvière Hill, on which can be found Roman ruins as well as a medieval pilgrimage chapel. Lyon has been famous for centuries for producing some of the most beautiful and luxurious silk cloth in the world, but for many its greatest claim to fame is its cuisine. Not just the Lyonnais (as the residents are known) but many visitors as well claim that the best food in France is found not in Paris but in Lyon.

Surrounding Lyon, and indeed up and down the river valleys of the region of eastern France known as Burgundy, can be found many of the most famous vineyards in the world. This area also contains a number of towns famous for a single product, such as the mustard-producing town of Dijon.

Located on the French Riviera, the city of Nice entices visitors with its temperate climate and sandy beaches.

The tiny independent principality of Monaco sits on the Mediterranean coast.

Another important regional landmark is the Rhine River, which serves as the border between France and Germany. Some of the fiercest fighting in modern European history has taken place between Germany and France over possession of this area because of its mineral and industrial wealth. As a result, the Alsace and Lorraine areas retain a strong Germanic streak in their culture, and indeed the names of cities like Strasbourg and Metz seem more German than French.

CENTRAL FRANCE

Though it lacks the marshes of the Camargue and the jagged peaks of the Alps, nearly everything else about the geography of France can be found in the central portion of the country. Among the most notable regions of the interior is the Auvergne. Its major city, Clermont-Ferrand, is an industrial center, but most of the Auvergne is strongly agricultural, producing some of the most popular cheeses in France. The Auvergne is part of the mountain range known as the Massif Central, a highland region containing some of the best grazing land in France. The region is distinguished by volcanic

CARCASSONNE

Looming over the plains of southwest France, Carcassonne, in the words of author Grace Coston in *Insight Guide: France*, is "without question the only medieval monument of its kind in Europe." In the nineteenth century, at the urging of famed French writer Prosper Mérimée, this medieval hilltop citadel was painstakingly restored, and today there is no other place that evokes so clearly the nature of medieval warfare and life under siege. Although the first ramparts were built in the Roman era, the current walls and buildings date from the time of the French king Louis IX, also known as Saint Louis, who undertook the project out of fear of a Spanish invasion. Later the four thousand residents of the town, and at least as many local villagers who took refuge inside its walls, endured a five-year siege by Charlemagne. The town proved impossible to take by force because it has two sets of defensive walls. Soldiers who crossed the first wall would find themselves easy prey for archers looking down from their safe hiding places in the second wall. Doors and other potential weak spots in the fortifications have spouts overhead for pouring scalding oil, and access to the city (other than by the many secret passages) is across a drawbridge complete with an iron gate. Inside the walls is a city complete with inns, shops, restaurants, a church, and the beautiful Château Comtal. A walk around the ramparts allows the visitor to take imaginary aim through arrow slits down into the narrow space between the walls, look down into narrow, crooked streets unchanged for hundreds of years, and enjoy beautiful panoramic views over the plains of Languedoc.

The walled city of Carcassonne, seen here at night, offers a glimpse into France's medieval past.

pillars called *puys,* which tower over the land below and sometimes, as in the city of Le Puy-en-Velay, are topped by religious monuments or chapels.

The other central region of particular note is the Loire Valley, south of Paris. Scattered along the river and in the nearby countryside are many beautiful chatêaus. From these, much of the history of France can be told. For example, the ruin at Chinon marks the spot where Joan of Arc proved to the crown prince's satisfaction that she had been sent by God to help him achieve his coronation in the middle of a war with England. In another part of the valley lies the huge royal hunting lodge at Chambord, known for its unique roof, with dozens of towers and chimneys resembling the skyline of a city. The king who ordered it built never even bothered to furnish most of the rooms and indeed never visited it in its completed state, a stark reminder of the excesses of the French monarchy.

The Loire Valley has attracted artists for several hundred years because of the beautiful light, which makes the river

A grape harvester works in one of Burgundy's many vineyards.

CORSICA

Officially part of France, Corsica is a Mediterranean island off the coast of Italy. Called Corsica, or "island of beauty," since ancient times, it has many interesting ruins from the Roman and other eras scattered among its rocky, mountainous landscapes. It is also well known for its vineyards, yielding some of the Mediterranean's best wines, and for its goat and sheep farming, which produces some excellent cheeses. It is also renowned for having some of the clearest blue water and most beautiful yet largely unspoiled beaches in the Mediterranean, and as a result it attracts many vacationers. In addition to water sports, vacationers can enjoy hiking in the Regional Nature Park on GR 20, one of France's many well-maintained footpaths, which traverses the rugged interior of the island.

Corsica's major city, Ajaccio, is a lively port filled with yachts particularly during the summer. But perhaps Ajaccio's greatest claim to fame is as the birthplace of Napoléon, who is commemorated all over the city, at his birthplace, in the church where he was baptized, and in several museums in buildings associated with his family, the Bonapartes.

and surrounding countryside shimmer with pastel colors. But it is only one of the limitless breathtaking regions of this remarkable country. In the nineteenth century artists such as Paul Gauguin gravitated to the colors and contrasts of Brittany and Provence. Others, such as Monet, Degas, and Toulouse-Lautrec, found their best subject matter in and around Paris. But whether an artist or not, wherever one goes in France it is easy to see the charm and magic of this most abundant of lands.

2

From Caves to Cathedrals: Prehistoric France Through the Middle Ages

Some of the best-preserved prehistoric art has been discovered in France, giving the world a better understanding of our common origins. However, the development of a distinct French identity rather than simply a human one only began to evolve centuries later, as a result of invasion and assimilation of a number of different peoples.

"Our Ancestors, the Gauls"

Humans have lived in the hexagonal area of modern France at least thirty-five thousand years, and earlier ancestors as far back as two million years B.C. By 18,000 B.C., cave dwellers were leaving behind drawings such as those in the Lascaux caves in the Dordogne region and the more recently discovered Cosquer cave near Marseille. By 5000 B.C., residents were creating stone monuments, which still dot the French landscape. It was not, however, until approximately 1000 B.C., that the first precursors of today's French people arrived on the scene.

They were the Celts, who also populated other parts of Europe and Great Britain. In France they are known as the Gauls, and every French schoolchild today is taught to refer to them as "our ancestors, the Gauls"[4] and to use the adjective Gallic to refer to long-standing French traditions and traits. With their fierce culture, the Gauls terrified their opponents by their habit of fighting naked, to show off their tattooed bodies. They also settled villages and grew crops, including grapes for the wine they traded along the major rivers of France and across the English Channel.

More is known about the Gauls than about previous groups primarily because of their contact with the ancient Romans. Emperor Julius Caesar, as well as noted Roman historians such as Germanicus, left behind written records of interactions with the Gauls, who were troublesome obstacles to the expansion of the Roman Empire into northern Europe. It is, in fact, from the Roman word "Galli" that the name "Gaul" comes. The Gauls themselves used tribal names such as the Parisii, from which the name of today's capital city is derived, and Arverni, which gave its name to the Auvergne.

ENTER THE ROMANS

Gallic aggressions tended to be small and localized, tied to control of farmland and trade routes. According to Robert Cole,

THE COSQUER CAVE

By far the most famous discovery of prehistoric art in France, the Lascaux caves, was made in 1940 at the small town of Montignac in Dordogne, by a boy looking for a lost dog. Fifty years later, in July 1991, an explorer of a different kind, also looking for something else, made a similarly startling find at Cape Morgiou, near Marseille. Scuba diver Jean Cosquer had a long-standing interest in cave diving, which involves exploring submerged tunnels in sea cliffs. He was not prepared for what he found at the end of one of these tunnels: a cave filled with drawings around eighteen thousand years old, from the same era as those of Lascaux. Fine examples of the whole range of painting styles of what is known as the Magdalenian era are found in the Cosquer cave, including stenciled hands and paintings of more than fifty species of animals, many now extinct.

The Cosquer cave (named after its discoverer) was probably about six miles inland at the time the paintings were done. Rising seawater at the end of the Ice Age sealed it off for millennia, thus preserving it from environmental and potential human damage. It is far less well known than Lascaux in part because almost no one is capable of visiting it because of the dangers of cave diving, and in part because it is smaller, has fewer paintings overall, and does not contain portable objects such as stone carvings. However, it is an important addition to our knowledge of the range of advanced human settlement in France, and a tantalizing reminder of what else remains to be discovered.

"None of the features of Celtic Gaul prepared its ruling peoples to compete with the Romans,"[5] who had a huge, well-organized army and a desire for world domination. Julius Caesar described his time in Gaul in three famous words: *"Veni, vidi, vinci"* ("I came, I saw, I conquered"). It was, in reality, not that simple. The Gallic Wars took seven years, from 58 to 51 B.C., because of the Gauls' unexpectedly strong resistance. According to historian Colin Jones, "Caesar's conquest was achieved with the loss of much [Gallic] blood. Battlefield losses and civilian massacres amounted to over a million dead, and it seems likely that between half a million and a million Gauls over the next decade were exported to the Italian peninsula, where they flooded the slave market."[6]

Though the Gallic Wars resulted in several centuries of subjugation at Roman hands, they are also the point at which the earliest glimmerings of a French identity began to take shape. This came in the person of an Arverni warrior named Vercingetorix, whose charismatic leadership united the discouraged Gauls and led to brief success against the Roman legions. His eventual defeat and capture at the siege of Alesia in 52 B.C. effectively ended organized resistance against the Romans. Vercingetorix was brought to Rome in chains and executed by strangulation, but his memory remains a source of pride even today.

Once the Gauls stopped warring with the Romans, their lives actually took a turn for the better. Indisputably, the Romans were a more advanced society, and during the period known as the Pax Romana (Roman Peace) they brought new technologies to Gaul, including roads and aqueducts, the remains of which can still be seen today. According to British journalist John Ardagh, "Julius Caesar had found Gaulish settlements made of wattle-and-daub [straw and mud]; several centuries of Roman rule produced . . . buildings in stone, brick, and marble."[7]

In about 1000 B.C., the Gauls invaded and settled the region known today as France.

VERCINGETORIX

Julius Caesar's own account of his exploits in Gaul, *The Gallic Wars*, contains an account of the rise of Vercingetorix, quoted here from Colin Jones's *Cambridge Illustrated History: France*. "Vercingetorix . . . a young Arverni with very great power in his tribe . . . called his dependants together and had no difficulty in rousing their passions. When it was known what he intended to do, there was a rush of armed men to join him. . . . He soon collected a large force of men [from many tribes], by urging them to take up arms in the cause of Gaulish freedom. . . . By general consent he was given the supreme command." Vercingetorix, whom Caesar called "a man of enormous energy," was the most important indigenous hero in the Gallic Wars, but only in later centuries were his motivations reinterpreted as a selfless desire for his people's freedom, or to a vision of a unified nation of Gauls. According to John Ardagh and Colin Jones in *Cultural Atlas of France*, "The great Arvernian warrior Vercingetorix . . . appears to have had some sense of 'national' unity, but this was probably the last throw of a desperate gambler rather than the program of an effective politician." To today's French, Vercingetorix's motivation is not as important as the fact that, for whatever reason, he is indisputably the first historical symbol of a united France.

Over time, Gallic identity all but disappeared. The religion of the Druids, the priests of the Gauls, was replaced by Christianity, and a great deal of intermarriage and cultural mixing took place, so that by the end of the Roman era, a new Gallo-Roman identity had been forged across much of France. Today the ancient Romans are viewed not as invaders but as an integral and even proud part of the history of the French people.

CLOVIS AND THE UNIFICATION OF FRANCE

Roman rule of Gaul lasted until the fourth century A.D., when Rome fell to invading Germanic tribes. In the aftermath, a power struggle ensued. Under an ambitious warrior king, Clovis, a group called the Franks, from just beyond the northern edge of Roman Gaul, were able to take the region for themselves. Preventing a Germanic conquest of Gaul proved to be of immense historic and cultural significance because blending such as that between the Romans and

Gauls never occurred, and the Germans and French have remained culturally and ethnically distinct to this day.

Clovis ruled from 481 to 511 and is considered the first king of the Frankish kingdom, from which the modern nation (and name) of France is derived. Clovis established a new capital in Paris, evidence that the new center of power was the north, not Roman Gaul. Clovis's sons continued the expansion, and by 600 Burgundy had become firmly part of the Frankish kingdom, and Aquitaine and Provence were at least loosely controlled. The boundaries of the Frankish kingdom were actually larger than the France of today, stretching from the English Channel and the Atlantic Coast to the Mediterranean, and as far into Germany as the present-day cities of Cologne and Mainz.

THE CAROLINGIAN DYNASTY

Inevitable disputes over power by Clovis's descendants led to a sectioning of the Frankish kingdom into realms ruled by different branches of the royal family. Gradually power slipped even from these rulers to powerful palace administrators not of the royal family, one of whom, Pépin, declared himself the new king of the Frankish kingdom and established the Carolingian dynasty, so named because several of the most important kings of this family were named Carolus, Latin for Charles.

Roman ruins, such as the Pont du Gard aqueduct, still exist in France today.

The first of these important kings named Charles was Charles Martel, Pépin's illegitimate son. A skilled general, "Charles the Hammer" is best known for his role in the Battle of Poitiers in northern Aquitaine in 732. Arab forces had conquered North Africa in the name of Islam and gone on to conquer Spain in 711. Since then they had pushed deep into France, threatening not just the political but also the religious foundations of the Frankish kingdom. Charles Martel defeated the Arabs so decisively at Poitiers that their advance in Europe was stopped.

The second important king named Charles was Charles the Great, or Charlemagne, who ruled from 768 to 814 and "extended Frankish authority over most of the Christian west."[8] On Christmas Day 800, Pope Leo III crowned Charlemagne emperor, a title no one had held

During the sixth century, Clovis (depicted here in battle) established Paris as the capital of the Frankish kingdom.

since Roman times. Only a person as talented and determined as Charlemagne could have kept the huge and unwieldy empire on course, for in the year 800 the Franks had no tradition of military and political organization like most of the Romans. Charlemagne made the rounds of the empire as best he could, and he appointed ministers whose main job was to monitor the loyalty of powerful nobles, but by the end of his reign it was already apparent that his empire would soon disintegrate as a result of ambitious nobles and new threats of invasion, this time from the Vikings, or Norsemen, of Scandinavia.

Charlemagne's son, Louis the Pious, officially acknowledged the inevitable splintering of his father's empire by announcing that upon his death the kingdom would be divided among his children. Family rivalries after his death in 840 were the downfall of the first united French kingdom. Although the Carolingians were able to hold on to royal titles and at least the superficial loyalty of the nobility, the balance of power had shifted decidedly toward dukes and other large landholders. Illustrating this shift in power are the late ninth-century words of the Bishop of Reims to the King of West

*Charles Martel halted
the advance of Arab
invaders during the
eighth century.*

Francia: "You have so many partners and equals in the kingdom that you reign more in name than in reality."[9]

By the mid-900s, the former empire of Charlemagne had
become, in the words of John Ardagh, "effectively a patchwork
of petty states, and the royal domain was restricted to a scrap
of land centered in the Île de France, measuring only some 200
by 100 kilometers."[10] The king was still powerful primarily because of traditional loyalty and respect for the role. This loyalty
was both formal and binding, part of a complex system known
as feudalism, one of the hallmarks of the Middle Ages (also
called the medieval era). Feudal kings granted land and titles,
such as Duke of Berry, to supporters—or sometimes rivals—in
exchange for a promise of perpetual loyalty and service. Over
the generations, however, descendants of the person who had
been given the land began to see it as their hereditary right

rather than a benefit presented to an ancestor out of the graciousness of a king, and though certain services and loyalty continued to be required of them, they behaved as if they were kings themselves, and sometimes even started using that title. Kings of France were at this point elected by the nobility, who cared little who won, because the monarch himself had little power or land.

THE CAPETIAN DYNASTY

Yet history takes many surprising turns, especially in France. The rise of Hugh Capet to the throne of West Francia in 987, and the founding of the Capetian dynasty, was to usher in a new period of rule by powerful kings. Hugh, a descendant of the Carolingian kings, was able to exert very little real power

THE NORMANS

Culture and history are shaped not only by conquerors and invaders, but also by successful resistance against them. Among those the French managed to ward off in their early history were Germanic tribes, the Arabs, and the Vikings. Also known as men of the north, or Norsemen, the Vikings began their spread from Scandinavia into Europe around A.D. 800. They soon began encroaching on the Frankish kingdom, but after a defeat in 911, the Viking leader Rollo struck a deal whereby he and his band would be allowed to settle and control the area around Rouen as a semiautonomous state, in exchange for an agreement to convert to Christianity and defend the area against any subsequent attacks by other Viking bands. Rollo's family and followers quickly became assimilated, marrying the children of local Frankish nobles, adopting Christian names and cultural practices, and identifying as Franks. Before long the people of the region were known as Normans (derived from the word *Norse*, or "North"), and their land became Normandy.

Rollo's descendants were to play a pivotal role in European history only a century after they first settled on Frankish lands. In 1066, William, a descendant of Vikings, who was now the Duke of Normandy, invaded and quickly conquered England. The Norman Conquest ushered in a momentous era of shifting loyalties and rivalries between France and England, and played an essential role in shaping English society and government along French lines for several centuries to come.

Charlemagne amassed an extensive Frankish empire during his forty-six-year reign.

himself during his nine-year reign, but he introduced the practice of crowning the heir before the death of the current king. The result was the establishment, because of the timely production of male heirs, of a continuing Capetian line, which put an effective end to elective kingship and sowed the seeds for a new, more powerful monarchy.

Hugh also understood the value of the king's connection with the Church. He saw to it that his son Robert II the Pious was crowned at Reims Cathedral in a solemn ceremony including invented rituals symbolizing a special relationship between the king and God. From then on the Capetian dynasty took great pains to promote the idea that kings are chosen by God, have the right to rule as they see fit, and are to be obeyed without question. Capetian links to the Church were reinforced by construction of many of France's finest Gothic-style religious buildings during this era, including the Abbey of Saint-Denis (where French kings were buried), Notre-Dame de Paris, and the cathedrals at Reims and Chartres.

CRUSADES AND CATHARS

To show that they also were powerful allies of the Church, French nobles scurried to raise armies when, in 1095, Pope Urban II announced a crusade to liberate the Holy Land from the Muslim group known as the Saracens. The Crusades strengthened the link in people's minds between God's will and the earthly power of kings and nobles, but the new equation of war with holiness would have tragic repercussions still deeply felt in the south of France today. In the twelfth century, the Cathars, or pure-living ones, a group centered in Languedoc near the town of Albi, preached their belief that God has no more power than the devil. They rejected the bureaucracy and practices of the Catholic Church, believing instead that the way to remain aligned with God in the battle between the two powers was to live an extremely simple life devoted to prayer and contemplation.

In 1208 Pope Innocent III decided that the crusade could be used against fringe Christians as well as against Muslims, and he called for a crusade to eradicate the Cathars. In support of the pope, the Capetian king Philip Augustus sent a

NOTRE-DAME DE PARIS

If Paris is the heart of France, the Cathedral of Notre Dame is the heart of Paris. The truth of this is underscored by the fact that all the national roads originating in Paris use the cathedral as the zero kilometer marker. Thus, for example, if one is at the two-hundred-kilometer mark on the road between Paris and Lyon, it means one is two hundred kilometers from Notre Dame.

People have worshiped at the site of the cathedral, an island in the middle of the Seine, for two thousand years, but it was not until 1163 that architect Maurice de Sully was commissioned to undertake construction of the present building in the Gothic style of the time, a task that ended up taking 150 years.

The cathedral has awed people throughout the centuries, with its 270-foot spire and graceful flying buttresses, which are curved pillars propping up the exterior walls at the front, or apse, of the church. The interior is spacious but quite dark, with little more than hundreds of prayer candles to dispel the gloom. At the time the cathedral was built, stone walls were not strong enough to support their weight as well as that of the roof if windows were too large. But the overall darkness of the church is offset by the remarkable rose window at the entrance to the cathedral, which forms a halo over a statue of the Virgin Mary, for whom the cathedral is named. The window's thirty-one-foot diameter made it one of the engineering marvels of its time, and its delicately patterned colored glass is some of the finest ever manufactured.

Near the entrance to the cathedral stands a row of headless statues of kings of Judah and Israel. Even though they did not depict French kings, their heads were knocked off during the French Revolution by zealous antimonarchists. Only recently were the heads found, and they are now on display at the nearby Cluny Museum. Framing the entrance to the cathedral are two towers, one housing the Bourdon, the sixteen-ton bell that Quasimodo rang in Victor Hugo's famous 1831 novel *Notre-Dame de Paris*, known in English as *The Hunchback of Notre Dame*.

Hugh Capet founded the Capetian dynasty, which produced a long line of powerful kings.

general named Simon de Montfort to destroy the Cathars and their supporters. The campaign against the Cathars was noted for its savagery, with the crowning incident occurring in 1245, when the last hideout of the Cathars, Montségur, in the foothills of the Pyrenees, was captured and in a single mass bonfire, two hundred Cathar men, women, and children were burned alive.

THE HUNDRED YEARS' WAR

Though the Capetians had managed to forge in the popular mind a link between their kingship and the will of God, in the early fourteenth century all this apparently meant was that God wished them to rule a tiny patch of land in the Île-de-France. Political alliances and shrewd marriages to heirs of large landholdings gradually brought much of the original Frankish kingdom back under their control. By the time the last Capetian king, Charles IV, died in 1328, West Francia had become a much larger kingdom, now known simply as Francia, or France, and its people the Francians, or French. Now, unlike in the past, when the king had little power and even less land, suddenly the nobles cared very much who the king was and what he did. But most important, the king now ruled with a more potent tool than anyone before him: the concept of divine right, holding that the monarch ruled by the will and with the blessing of God.

Though the foundation had been laid for a powerful monarchy, this in fact would have to wait a while longer. Within ten years the new ruling family, the Valois, who came to power only because Charles IV died without a direct male heir, would find themselves embroiled in the complex territorial disputes and political turmoil known as the Hundred Years' War. The Valois claim to the throne was not particularly strong, and in 1337, sensing the need to take decisive action to show he had the right to rule, King Philip VI confiscated

Aquitaine, which had come under English control by marriage. King Edward IV of England immediately invaded France and claimed not only Aquitaine but the French throne as well. Thus began the Hundred Years' War.

The name implies an ongoing battle between two clearly defined sides, France and England, but this is not an accurate picture. The French nobility did not want an English

THE FIRST UNIVERSITIES

Before the twelfth century, the only existing schools were those used to educate priests in Latin and theology, and the priesthood was often the best life choice for younger sons who would not inherit their fathers' land. However, as the Capetian dynasty consolidated its power and government bureaucracy increased, and as cities (and the need for services in them) grew, men who might otherwise have gone into the Church began to choose careers in medicine, law, and government administration. For all of these they needed formal learning of a different type than that offered by the Church. In Paris and in regional centers as well, such as Montpellier, Toulouse, and Avignon, centers of learning sprung up to spread this new knowledge, although in the beginning these centers were little more than followings of a single teacher of renown, such as Pierre Abélard (1079–1142), whose alternative school in a Paris cloister soon was more popular than the cathedral school of Notre Dame.

With this new demand for higher education, these centers grew into permanent institutions closely linked with the Church, but with their own buildings and faculty. One of the first French universities was in Montpellier, renowned for its medical school, but the most famous university was the University of Paris, which had its beginning with Abélard. So great was the need for educated young men that another famous Parisian university, the Sorbonne, named for its founder Robert de Sorbon, was set up nearby to educate bright young men of humble birth who could not otherwise afford schooling.

As John Ardagh and Colin Jones point out in *Cultural Atlas of France*, "The young men who formed the student population were a cosmopolitan, footloose, boisterous crowd, particularly in Paris," and cities with universities were known for their lively social, intellectual, and cultural life, especially near where the students lived. The Left Bank of Paris today is a student quarter dating from medieval times.

JOAN OF ARC

Joan of Arc is one of the best-known people in French history, but her personality and her role remain as puzzling today as they were in her time. Joan was born around 1412 in Domrémy, a small village in Lorraine. When she was thirteen she started hearing voices and seeing visions of saints, who told her to bring the dauphin, or crown prince, across enemy lines to Reims where he could be crowned. At Chinon she convinced the dauphin of her mission when she recognized him, disguised in a crowd, by a vision of a golden crown over his head. Remarkable as it may seem, troops that Joan led were able to break the Siege of Orléans, thus returning the city of Reims to French hands and clearing the way for coronation of the dauphin as Charles VII. Once this was accomplished, Charles had no further use for this strange young girl who cut her hair and dressed in men's styles, and who emphatically insisted on her voices and her visions. When rumors intensified that Joan was a witch, a heretic, and a sorcerer, he grew nervous that his connection to her might weaken his already somewhat shaky hold on the throne, so he allowed her to be turned over to the English, who burned her at the stake at Rouen in 1431 at the age of nineteen.

Just what role Joan played at the Siege of Orléans is not completely clear. She was prominently and visibly there, but probably played a supporting and symbolic role rather than that of a military strategist and general. Her insistence that she directly spoke with saints did not sit well first with the

Catholic Church, who wanted to be the only link between people and God, and then with the people of later centuries who found such claims irrational and unnerving. It was not until the nineteenth century that Joan emerged as a national hero.

Joan of Arc became a French heroine for her role in France's victory at the Siege of Orléans.

king, but they did not want a strong French one cutting into their power either, and they saw the disarray of the Hundred Years' War as a way of increasing their independence. A noble's loyalty for the most part existed only to himself at this point, and alliances shifted according to convenience. The Hundred Years' War could more accurately be called simply a hundred years of war, characterized by isolated skirmishes between small, local armies, and general plundering all over France, rather than by a series of big battles and strong coordination at the national level.

After nearly a hundred years of warfare, the French gained the upper hand with the decisive defeat of English forces at the Siege of Orléans.

The Siege of Orléans

Still, at the heart of the conflict was the question of who the rightful French king was and what land he legitimately controlled. By the last few decades of the war, the south was securely in French hands, but the north, including Paris, was held by England, then in alliance with the powerful duke of Burgundy. The tide of the war would turn decisively for the French in the early 1400s with the appearance of an unlikely hero, a young peasant girl named Joan of Arc. Joan had visions of angels telling her that she needed to take the dauphin, the crown prince of France, to Reims (then under English control), where he could be officially crowned king. Joan was at the forefront of the great 1429 French victory at the Siege of Orléans, followed by a dazzling coronation of the dauphin as King Charles VII. The French firmly had the upper hand at this point, and in 1453, the English conceded defeat. The Hundred Years' War was over, signaling the end of the medieval era.

Torn and Reborn: The Early Modern Era

France was in ruins at the end of the Hundred Years' War. A century of plundering and destruction had created famine and intolerable living conditions. One resident of Normandy wrote that "from Dieppe to Rouen there is not a recognizable track left; there are no farms and, with the exception of a few bandits, no men."[11] But this was not the worst of what the country had faced. Between 1348 and 1352, the first and worst of the epidemics known as the Black Death killed approximately one-third of the people of Europe. But for all their damage, war and plague also presented opportunities to build a different, and perhaps improved, society.

The End of Feudalism

France had been at war so long that no one alive remembered the way things were before, and the plague killed so many heads of families and leading members of society that those who lived faced total social chaos. One thing was clear, however: The feudal system, built on bonds of loyalty and mutual assistance, was dead. By the end of the Hundred Years' War in 1453, kings no longer wanted armies supplied on demand by dukes and counts. They wanted permanent armies of professional soldiers loyal only to them. New taxes known as the *taille* were enacted to pay for an army that would answer only to the king, a development that would strengthen the power of the king.

Nobles became more interested in having money to fight among themselves and to buy the luxuries they wanted. They began permitting serfs to earn money by working as skilled laborers outside the estate. With their new wages, the serfs, who had been legally bound to their lords' estates and were virtually slaves, were able to use the money to buy their freedom. Once free, people moved to towns, forming a small, independent

Victims of the Black Death, the deadly plague that decimated a third or more of the people of Europe, receive care at a Parisian hospital.

middle class. These towns were unsanitary and crowded, and the Black Death hit them hard, but those who survived found that they lived better than ever—even after paying mounting taxes—because their skills were in so much demand.

Paying taxes instead of continually providing service was a profound shift. People in towns no longer felt any identification with or loyalty to the local lord. Town councils and trade guilds flourished. At court, the nobles demanded as a condition of their continued loyalty that they be allowed to interpret and enforce the king's laws in their own way on their own lands, and that the nobles be consulted on matters of importance to them. From these changes in attitude gradually emerged the first parliaments and the first systems of local governance under a framework of national law.

THE WARS OF RELIGION

Within a few decades of the end of the Hundred Years' War, French cities had once again become bustling centers for the arts, commerce, and industry. Yet, wherever people congregated, new tensions arose. The Protestant Reformation, which began in Germany in 1517, was initially quite popular in France, but soon it became a divisive force. Catholics saw Protestantism as a heresy. Protestants preferred the new emphasis on a direct relationship with God through prayer and Bible reading to subservience to a Catholic Church whose clergy were often corrupt and greedy.

Some of the nobles, however, saw the new religious movement as having the potential to shift the balance of political power. If Protestantism became the dominant faith, they

THE BLACK DEATH

Few deaths can be more agonizing than those from bubonic plague. When the first swellings, or buboes, occurred in the armpits and groin, the unlucky victim knew death was at hand within a day or two. Fever and cramps followed, then the buboes broke open and the victim soon died. By then people living in the same house were likely to begin to see signs of swelling on their own bodies, and the cycle repeated itself until whole families, and sometimes whole towns, were wiped out. Corpses piled up outside houses, to be collected onto carts and taken for mass burial or burning, until there was no one left to bury, or no one well enough to operate the carts.

Medicine was useless, and the death rate was almost 100 percent of those afflicted. One chronicle of the time, reported by Colin Jones in *Cambridge Illustrated History: France*, said that the only advice doctors could offer was to "leave early, go far, and come back late." But regardless of where one fled, the Black Death was likely to be there. One-third or more of the population of Europe was killed by plague, and in some regions the death rate was much higher. According to Jones, "Limoges was said to be down to its last five inhabitants in 1435."

No one understood how disease was transmitted, so wild theories abounded. Some said that the plague was God's vengeance on an evil society, and groups known as flagellants began wandering the countryside beating their own backs with whips and sticks to show their penitence. Others, looking for scapegoats, said that the Jews had poisoned water supplies, or that Mongols had deliberately catapulted infected bodies into port cities they were trying to capture. The disease was in fact brought from Asia by the overland silk routes, and by sea, where it was transmitted by bites from fleas that came from rats that jumped on and off ships and caravans.

reasoned, the current Catholic monarchy would fall. Approximately half the French nobility converted to Protestantism, creating intense political jockeying at court, which was soon reflected in violence in the streets. Between 1562 and 1598, eight "wars of religion" were fought. The worst atrocity was the 1572 St. Bartholomew's Eve Massacre, in which twenty-seven hundred Protestants in Paris and more than twenty thousand across the rest of France were murdered by angry mobs. A strong monarch might have been able to gain control of the situation, but France did not have one.

The death of King Henry III in 1589 prompted a series of suspicious deaths and known assassinations among Catholics vying for the throne. Within a few months the first Protestant king of France, Henry IV, was crowned. Henry would prove to be the capable leader France needed. Taking the situation in hand, he converted to Catholicism, declaring peace in Paris to be "worth a mass."[12] He did not support radical Catholics, however, and with the Edict of Nantes in 1598, he officially established freedom of religion in France. Many remained dissatisfied with the king's approach, and in the end he paid with his life, murdered by a fanatic named Ravaillac in 1610. Tensions between Protestants and Catholics continued to spill over in the towns and villages during the reign of Henry IV's successor, Louis XIII, while at court a wily nobleman who was also a high official in the Catholic Church, Cardinal Richelieu, took advantage of Louis's youth to promote Catholic interests and his own role as a royal adviser. Louis XIII's successor, Louis XIV, ended the turmoil in 1685 decisively by revoking the Edict of Nantes, sending 250,000 Huguenots (as French Protestants were called) into exile and entrenching Catholicism as the religion of France.

Henry IV established religious tolerance in France through the Edict of Nantes in 1598.

THE SUN KING

Louis XIV began his long reign in 1643, when he was only five years old. Louis XIV, or the Sun King, as he liked to be called, is probably best known for shifting the royal residence from

Versailles

According to Robert Cole in *A Traveler's History of France*, "Versailles was more than a home for King Louis. It was a symbol of French glory and unity, and of royal mastery over the forces of disorder." Its ten thousand rooms and miles of landscaped grounds took more than thirty-six thousand people and several decades to build. Today it astonishes visitors, much as it must have awed the king's guests, with its opulent decor in gold, marble, crystal, velvet, silk, and other materials that emphasized the bottomless wealth of the king. The Hall of Mirrors is one of its most famous rooms. It is a long gallery with windows on one side and mirrors on the other, which flood the room with light reflecting off the gilded window frames. At night the crystal chandeliers were lit with candles, giving Louis a glittering corridor through which to walk with his court and guests. The king's and queen's quarters are both lavishly decorated with gold and crystal, as well as with sumptuous tapestries and gold brocade bed canopies. The court was kept aware of its station by its cramped quarters elsewhere in the palace. The king even had his own theater for the ballets and operas he loved. In fact, it was his skill and interest in dancing that led to the development of ballet as an art form.

The grounds at Versailles are as magnificent as the palace. The porch of the palace looks out onto manicured gardens and immense flower beds. At the far end of these gardens is Apollo's Pool, from which a team of golden horses driven by a muscular Apollo rises through powerful jets of water. Beyond this is the Grand Canal, crossed at its midpoint by the Petit Canal, around which are huge stretches of lawn, punctuated by small groves and gardens designed to amuse and give some privacy to residents and guests. Parts of the grounds were kept wild for hunting, one of the favorite pastimes of royalty. A century later, Marie Antoinette would have her own little fake village built on one remote part of the grounds, where she and her friends could amuse themselves by pretending to be milkmaids or shepherdesses (although well-dressed ones with servants).

Versailles's magnificent Hall of Mirrors continues to awe visitors today.

the Louvre, in Paris, to the Palace of Versailles, twenty-three kilometers away. Building Versailles was a shrewd move on several levels. No longer could the nobles both live in their own homes in Paris and stay in regular contact with Louis. To see and be seen, they had to take up residence in his palace, and thus they were always in his shadow and under his watchful eye. In time a court culture evolved around menial services to the king. One noble might be honored by the privilege of handing the king his shirt in the morning, and another by the right to announce that the king's meal had arrived. People once more powerful than the king had become humble servants.

Supporting Louis's extravagances was extraordinarily expensive to the people of France, and his often reckless minor foreign wars increased the size of the bill their taxes paid. Discontent grew into revolts in the countryside. A growing middle class in the cities, more literate and better informed than ever as a result of the many newspapers and books now available, began to question the entire structure of French society, wondering aloud why the obvious riches of the country seemed to benefit so few. Likewise at court, discontent was brewing among the nobles, who resented their loss of importance. The Estates General, previously established to advise the king, was simply not convened any more. Regional *parlements*, or assemblies, had lost the power to lodge protests with the king. There seemed to be no one else in France ex-

Louis XIV ruled as an absolute monarch for more than seventy years.

cept Louis XIV. "L'état, c'est moi" ("I am the state"), he once said, implying that everything important filtered through or originated in him.

Louis reigned for over seventy years. No one challenged his power while he lived, but when he died in 1715, it quickly became clear that "Louis XIV had postured as an absolute ruler but he could not control posterity. . . . There was almost open rejoicing on the news of his death, and his reputation plummeted before he was cold in his grave."[13] His will was annulled by the same *parlement* of nobles he had ignored and suppressed. It also appointed Louis XIV's enemy the duke of Orléans to serve as regent for Louis's five-year-old great grandson, the new king. Acting for the king, the duke used his power to undo many of Louis XIV's edicts and limit the new king's power.

Louis XV also ruled a long time, dying in 1774. His reign was characterized by "personal mediocrity"[14] but his era, the Enlightenment, was one of the most glorious in French history. The emphasis of Enlightenment thinkers, known as *philosophes*, was on logic and reason, and belief in the existence of a god who gave people intelligence and then left them to govern themselves. This further undermined a monarchy built on the idea that kings were chosen by God, who oversaw and approved their every act. The middle class was also growing in size and in confidence. Businesses were flourishing, trade was growing, and the standard of living for the middle class was rising. Versailles became the symbol not of the king's importance, but of his isolation on the margins of the real life of the country. Nobles and wealthy commoners now treasured invitations to parties and salons held by prominent socialites more than they did invitations to court, and "the court [gave] way to the coffee house"[15] as the heart of French political life.

Louis XVI inherited the throne at a time of civil unrest in France.

The French Revolution and Its Aftermath

Louis XVI, the last king of the ancient régime, as the period before the French Revolution is known, inherited a realm on the verge of open revolt. Most of the population lived in cramped, unsanitary hovels in a state of near starvation, which they blamed on the diversion of massive amounts of money to support the king's lifestyle. Author Ardagh elaborates: "Hunger now fused with anger to create a revolutionary situation."[16] In 1788, to defuse the situation, Louis convened the Estates General for the first time since 1614. Tensions boiled over when the elected delegates of the Third Estate, the common people, were informed that although they were 96 percent of the population and held most of the seats, they would have only one-third of the say—the same as the nobility or the clergy, the other two estates. They refused to participate until the body was reconvened as a National Assembly with each delegate having one vote. Then, on July 14, 1789, while struggles over representation in the Estates General continued, a Paris mob stormed the Bastille, a prison symbolizing political oppression and a major arsenal for the crown, starting the French Revolution. Violence spread to the countryside; châteaus and church properties were burned and looted and their inhabitants attacked in a time known as the "Great Fear."

In the midst of the chaos, the National Assembly issued the famous "Declaration of the Rights of Man," abolishing any special privileges of the nobility and clergy in favor of equal treatment under the law for all citizens. But a radical element, made bold by their own power and by their sense that they were acting in a righteous cause, took control of the Assembly. Their hatred of the monarchy led to the eventual arrest of the king who, after an unsuccessful attempt to flee the country with his family, was beheaded by guillotine in

Angry Parisians storm the Bastille prison, igniting the French Revolution.

THE ENLIGHTENMENT

The church as a central focus of French life never fully recovered from the wars of religion. An increasingly skeptical society focused more on personal betterment on Earth, and on scientific explanations for matters that had once been taken on faith. The great scientific leaps of the seventeenth century, such as Newton's laws of physics, and the development of the scientific method itself, excited French intellectuals of the eighteenth century, known as *philosophes*, who saw how the spirit of scientific inquiry, which had done so much to explain the natural and physical world, might be applied to understanding human society. They were confident that the human mind was strong and versatile enough to reason through and solve all the problems of human society, but that superstition and ignorance, coupled with reliance on kings and priests, stood in the way. In a letter to Voltaire, the most eminent social critic of the era and author of *Candide* and other satires, quoted in Colin Jones's *Cambridge Illustrated History: France*, Diderot, author of a massive thirty-five-volume encyclopedia, wrote that the philosophes would have "no quarter for the superstitious, the fanatical, the ignorant, or for fools, malefactors or tyrants. I would like to see our brethren united in zeal for truth, goodness, and beauty. . . . We must show that science has done more for humankind than divine . . . grace."

The era of the philosophes, known as the Enlightenment, or the Age of Reason, produced many writers in a variety of disciplines. In addition to Diderot and Voltaire, leaders of the Enlightenment include Montesquieu, a political scientist, and Jean-Jacques Rousseau, whose autobiography, *Confessions*, used his personal stories to criticize the society of his time. Rousseau's belief that humans are born with limitless potential, which is crushed by society as they grow, struck a particular chord with readers. "Man is born free but everywhere he is in chains," he wrote in his famous *Social Contract*, a sentiment that would be echoed not only by French revolutionaries, but also by Romantic poets and thinkers of the following century.

1793, along with his wife, Marie Antoinette, who was widely despised for her indifference to the plight of the common people.

The anger unleashed among the citizenry in the aftermath of these executions, a time known as the Reign of Terror, has created lasting images of crowds roaring their approval as noble heads dropped into a blood-drenched basket at the base of the guillotine. The French people had a great deal to be angry about; for centuries they had produced the riches of the land while others reaped most of the benefit. But the real blood lust was centered in the new government itself. Swayed by the fanaticism of its leaders, George-Jacques Danton and Maximilien du Robespierre, the Convention, as the Assembly was now known, began capriciously sentencing Parisians to death on the vague charge of betraying the revolution; there was no possibility of appeal. The figure of twenty thousand dead in the fifteen-month period now known as the Reign of Terror is frequently cited, but it is probably too high. Nevertheless, whether by firing squad to quell rural riots or by beheading in Paris, death was common. According to Robert Cole, "Equality of a sort had been achieved: no one was safe . . . neither aristocrat nor commoner, guilty or innocent."[17]

NAPOLÉON

The guillotine in the Place de la Concorde became the main symbol of a revolution gone wrong. The atrocities committed against the French people there were worse than those of any French king in history. Robespierre himself was guillotined in 1794, when people finally began to question the inconsistency of the Convention's tactics with the belief in human rights, which had given birth to it. Though the executions then stopped, the new government, called the Directory, was ineffective at establishing order. Gangs terrorized Paris and the countryside, and the army was often brought in to quell riots.

A brash young officer charged with riot control would rise to become one of the most important figures in world history. Napoléon Bonaparte was rewarded in 1796 for his effectiveness with Paris mobs by being given command of the French army in Italy. Though his charge was simply to tie up Prussian troops in Italy while a battle was fought on another front, he stunned everyone by conquering Italy altogether. His military brilliance abroad was welcomed but his unwillingness to follow orders alarmed the cautious Directory, which summoned him home for discipline. Napoléon had other plans. He overthrew the Directory at gunpoint and had himself declared First Consul of the Republic.

Napoléon's decisive style was just what the weary and frightened people of France were looking for. He moved quickly to confirm the rights gained in the revolution and established a uniform system of law called the Napoleonic Code. He stopped the decline of the economy and restored order by ruthlessly suppressing public unrest. In 1804, he declared himself emperor, a seemingly unthinkable move in a land that had recently arrested, imprisoned, and decapitated its monarch. But Napoléon was an international sensation and hero whose success affirmed the principle of human potential at the heart of the Enlightenment. For a while at least, the grander his ambition, the more France admired and supported him.

Napoléon declared himself emperor of France in 1804.

Napoléon's desires reached far beyond the confines of France. He launched campaigns to unseat or force into alliance the other royal families of Europe, and he was successful everywhere on the continent for several years, winning famous battles at Marengo and Austerlitz, among others. The only power he could not subdue was Great Britain. A French blockade of British ports backfired when the British counterblockade isolated French ports, sending the national economy into decline. Sensing weakness, various countries began conspiring against Napoléon. In 1812 Napoléon invaded Russia, a disastrous adventure in which his invading force of six hundred thousand was reduced to less than ninety thousand.

Napoléon was forced to abdicate in 1814 when, in the ultimate humiliation, the czar of Russia invaded Paris and the French monarchy was restored under Louis XVIII. Napoléon was exiled to Elba, a small Mediterranean island, where he stayed only one year before he was encouraged by his supporters to return to Paris. In a period known as the Hundred

NAPOLÉON BONAPARTE: ROMANTIC HERO

Napoléon Bonaparte is without a doubt one of the most influential and important figures of Western history. Still, nothing about his background would lead one to expect great things of him. He was born in Ajaccio, Corsica, on August 15, 1769, to Charles-Marie Bonaparte, a lawyer, and his wife, Letizia Romolino. His father died when Napoléon was young, and the child was sent to military school in Brienne, France. From there he entered into military service, rising to the rank of brigadier general by age twenty-four as a result of his role in forcing the retreat of the British fleet at Toulon. Assigned to an artillery patrol in Paris, he opened cannon fire (which he famously called "a whiff of grape shot") at point-blank range on demonstrators trying to break up the National Convention, killing and wounding hundreds. This audacity brought him to the attention of his superiors, who arranged to have him sent to Italy in 1796 to lead a military campaign there. Historians and psychologists debate exactly what this man possessed that made him not settle at that point into a rather dull and predictable military career, but rather return to Paris and establish himself as France's ruler by the barrel of a gun, then go on to build an empire to rival Charlemagne's. No explanation seems adequate, but the spirit of the times, known as the Romantic era, encouraged common people to believe in their dreams and their capabilities. Napoléon became the prime example of such self-confidence. He was the hero of many Romantic writers, and composer Ludwig Beethoven dedicated his Third Symphony, "Eroica," to him (although he tore up the dedication when Napoléon declared himself emperor). Whatever else Napoléon was, he was a person perfectly suited to his time. "If it only lasts," his mother was heard to sigh when advised that her son had crowned himself emperor of France. Perhaps in the end she may have felt it did not, but today Napoléon Bonaparte is one of the most enduring figures in world history—in the words of Robert Cole in *A Traveler's History of France*, "an egoist who left a psychological mark upon France greater than any figure before or since."

From inauspicious beginnings, Napoléon rose to become one of the most influential figures in Western history.

Days, Louis XVIII fled, and Napoléon resumed power. In 1815 he was roundly defeated by allied European forces at the Battle of Waterloo in Belgium, then forced into permanent exile.

In the years that followed, France swung wildly between monarchy and republics run by elected governments. One noteworthy leader of the era was Louis Philippe. He survived seventeen assassination attempts in his eighteen-year reign, known as the July Monarchy, before he was overthrown in 1848 when a pro–working-class Second Republic was declared. The legislature of the Second Republic shortened working days and extended the right to vote to all adult males, but for many this was not enough, and revolts again broke out in 1848.

A popular nephew of Napoléon, Louis Napoléon, was then elected president. Though in 1851 he declared himself emperor, as his uncle had, arresting all who opposed him, surprisingly he was able to stay in power almost twenty years. He was helped by generally strong economic conditions and by his commissioning of Baron Georges Haussmann to remodel central Paris. The new grand boulevards such as the Champs-Élysées and beautiful public parks such as the Bois de Boulogne created a sense of civic pride that enhanced the emperor's prestige. He brought about his own downfall, however, in the Franco-Prussian War and was forced to abdicate when France was defeated at Sedan in 1870.

Louis Philippe survived seventeen assassination attempts during his eighteen-year reign.

After their country's defeat in war, angry workers tired of having national resources squandered established the Paris Commune, an attempt at a government by the working class. The government reacted violently. When the final Commune members were gunned down at Paris's Père Lachaise Cemetery after a two-month siege, the total dead numbered over twenty thousand French killed by other French. Demoralized and confused by their seeming inability to create a stable, long-term system of government, and by the amount of blood that had been shed in the past century, the French watched and waited for what the new Third Republic would bring.

FRANCE IN THE MODERN ERA

After the fall of Louis Napoléon, France had to come to grips with the fact that its status as a European power had dwindled along with its size and that its internal problems were severe. Even the first president of the Third Republic, Adolphe Thiers, "gave the infant republic little chance of survival."[18] The early move of the Third Republic to put down unrest by destroying the Paris Commune killed thousands more people at government hands in one week than the entire Reign of Terror had. This horror came on the heels of a humiliating German occupation of Paris at the end of the Franco-Prussian War, demonstrating that the powerful France of Charlemagne and Napoléon had been brought to its knees both internally and internationally. A deeply demoralized nation wondered if the future could have anything good in store. Yet France is full of surprises. The Third Republic brought prosperity and growth, and "escorted France confidently into the twentieth century."[19]

For the next several generations, French people lived free from bloodshed at home and abroad. During the Third Republic, which lasted seventy years, France managed for the first time to have a democratic form of government that did not come apart over political disagreements. Though the Third Republic was politically turbulent on the surface—approximately sixty changes in leadership took place between 1870 and 1914—a clearer understanding grew among both politicians and the general public that working together and compromise are essential to a democracy and that, in the words of Thiers, the best government will be the one which "divides us the least."[20]

A CHANGING SOCIETY

Divisions remained deep, however, between cities and countryside, between provincial and national identities, between the church and the government, and between the comfortable

THE DREYFUS AFFAIR

In 1894 a cleaning lady emptying the trash in the German embassy in Paris noticed a piece of paper which appeared to indicate that an unknown French army officer was actually a German spy. Suspicion soon fell on Captain Alfred Dreyfus, a thirty-five-year-old staff officer to a French general. A trial quickly followed, and Dreyfus was convicted of treason and sentenced to Devil's Island, a notorious prison colony off the coast of South America, despite the very weak evidence against him and his continued protestations of innocence.

The Dreyfus trial developed into one of the great scandals and political causes of its time because it became apparent that the army was covering up evidence pointing to another man, and allowing the only Jewish officer on the general's staff to be a scapegoat. Anti-Semitism has had a long and ugly history in Europe, and France is no exception. According to Colin Jones in *Cambridge Illustrated History: France*, "It was to cries of 'Dirty Jew!' and 'Down with Jews' from the watching crowds that Dreyfus was formally stripped of his military rank," and known anti-Semitic newspapers rallied in support of his conviction even as evidence of his innocence mounted.

Leading the efforts to clear Dreyfus was novelist and essayist Émile Zola, whose famous essay "J'Accuse" ("I Accuse") laid out the issues to the French public in an open letter to the newspaper *L'Aurore* in 1898. Dreyfus was eventually released from prison with a pardon in 1899, but his name was not actually cleared until 1906. A loyal French citizen and military man (his words as he was sent to prison were simply, "Long live France! Long live the Army!"), he rejoined the army to fight in World War I and received the Legion of Honor award for his service.

French army officer Alfred Dreyfus was convicted of treason against France.

Provençal poet Frédéric Mistral, pictured here with his wife, led a movement to renew pride in the local culture.

middle class and the poor. While life was steadily improving for the middle class, the government largely ignored the problems of the working class, resulting in the growth of left-wing labor movements uniting factory workers and farmers. Added to this was a rekindling of regional pride, fostered by such leaders as Provençal poet Frédéric Mistral. Pride in local culture often became equated with antigovernment sentiments, and people became more and more determined to force an unresponsive government to listen.

The Third Republic, however, focused instead on promoting a single French identity and support for a strong central government. In measures introduced by President Jules Ferry between 1881 and 1886, schooling became mandatory for all boys and girls between age six and thirteen, and vast sums of money were put into building and staffing public schools. Curriculum was specifically focused on French history and other topics promoting French identity and pride. French was the only language allowed; use of regional languages, even on the playground, was discouraged and in many cases punished.

Whatever the government's motives—and despite their continued indifference to appalling work and living conditions among the miners, factory workers, and other laborers in France—its emphasis on public schooling is one of the Third Republic's great achievements. By the early twentieth century, France had a literacy rate of 90 percent. However, increased literacy only highlighted some of the problems the Third Republic had struggled to keep under wraps. Newspaper circulation skyrocketed, and people became more involved with political issues and social causes, including antigovernment ones. The treason trial of a French army officer, Captain Alfred Dreyfus, in 1894, for example, exploded into a national scandal as a result of newspaper coverage and exposed deep divisions in French life and politics.

LA BELLE ÉPOQUE

The latter half of the nineteenth century up until World War I is often referred to as La Belle Époque (which roughly translates as "the beautiful era") in France. The center of the Belle Époque was Paris, which had become a dazzling display of technological marvels such as gas and electric lighting, consumer indulgences such as big department stores, engineering advances such as widened streets and public transportation, and architectural marvels such as the Eiffel Tower. Constructed for the 1889 Universal Exhibition, the tower (which many people thought a monstrosity at the time) quickly became a beloved symbol of all that was new and exciting about life in Paris.

Middle-class people in Paris as a whole lived, ate, and dressed better than their fellow citizens. Indeed, with indoor plumbing, running water, and electric and gas service in their homes, they lived far better than even royalty had in the past. But by far the most characteristic aspect of the era was the explosion in the number of things typical middle-class Parisians, with more money in their pockets than ever before, could do in their leisure time. The famous Moulin Rouge music hall, home of the cancan, opened in Paris in 1889, followed by the Folies Bergère (a music hall and variety theater) and the Paris Casino. Those wishing to leave Paris could now take the train for a weekend in fashionable resorts such as Deauville, on the west coast of France, or take a longer trip to the French Riviera. The relative ease of train travel revived the medieval pilgrimage as a more somber form of holiday, and the town of Lourdes became the destination of over a half-million visitors a year. Organized sports also grew in popularity, the most famous of which is the Tour de France, an overland bicycle race that was first held in 1903.

The Moulin Rouge music hall opened during France's Belle Époque.

COLONIAL EXPANSION

Jules Ferry changed France with his emphasis on schooling, but he changed the world with his views on colonization. At the beginning of the twentieth century, European powers were involved in a scramble to establish colonies in Africa and southern Asia. Ferry saw overseas colonies as essential to French economic growth and world power. France, which had a colony in Algeria already, added Tunisia as a protectorate in 1881. This was followed by colonies in Southeast Asia, in West Africa, and in the Pacific.

WORLD WAR I

By the beginning of the century, France's colonial empire was the second largest in the world, and France was feeling revived and powerful both at home and abroad. These feelings were soon overshadowed by growing worries about a new emphasis on the military in Germany. Then in 1914 a complex series of events, beginning with the assassination in the Balkan city of Sarajevo of Archduke Ferdinand of Austria drew all Europe into war. Because of their shared border, France squared off against Germany in what the French thought would be a quick and decisive victory.

The conflict developed into a war of attrition lasting four years, with battles fought over the same few square miles of territory over and over again, and hundreds of thousands of lives sacrificed for what often seemed to be little apparent reason. New technologies made the war particularly horrible. Mustard gas was used against thousands of combatants, who died choking on their own blood in muddy or frozen trenches. The newly invented airplane was used to bomb ground troops, forever changing the dynamics of war. In one campaign alone, at Verdun, France suffered 700,000 casualties, part of the astronomical total of approximately 1.5 million French soldiers killed and another 3 million wounded in the war.

When the Germans admitted defeat in 1918, the French government tried to paint the result as yet another great military triumph for the descendants of Vercingetorix, Charles Martel, and Joan of Arc. The decade of the 1920s, known in France as "les années folles" (the crazy years), seemed light-hearted and confident on the surface, but the devastation of the war, a lengthy depression, and the increasingly obvious

French soldiers lead an offensive attack at Verdun during World War I.

plight of the poor gave it a somber undercurrent. Tensions heightened between groups on the far Left and Right, but neither could gain enough support to govern effectively, or for very long. France seemed adrift, unsure how to address its problems or chart its future.

WORLD WAR II

Meanwhile, Germany was under the sway of a charismatic politician named Adolf Hitler. At another time France might have seen quickly and clearly the threat he presented, but many French feared a workers' revolution such as the one in Russia, which had put Communists in power. To them Hitler's anti-Communist stance seemed like a good thing for Europe, and his obvious preparations for war went unchallenged by the French government.

World War II was touched off by the German invasion of Poland in the fall of 1939, and France was invaded a few months later, in May 1940. Completely unprepared for Germany's new "blitzkrieg" style of simultaneous air and ground force assault, by June 1940 huge numbers of French and British soldiers had been pushed across northern France by German forces, and were saved from annihilation only by the heroic efforts of British fishermen who evacuated the soldiers on their boats a few at a time from the beach at Dunquerque (Dunkirk).

Around the same time, the French government, along with nearly 2 million Parisians, fled from Paris in the face of an imminent German occupation. Soon after, France was divided into northern and southern regions; the Germans occupied the north, including Paris, and a puppet French government, under World War I hero Marshal Philippe Pétain, oversaw the administration of French law from the resort town of Vichy, under the thumb of the Germans. The Third Republic had ended, and one of the most traumatic eras in French history had begun. With scarcely a fight, France had fallen in war. It was, according to historian Marc Bloch, "the most terrible collapse in all the long story of our national life."[21]

COLLABORATION AND RÉSISTANCE

The goal of the Vichy government was to sweep away ideas such as democracy, political inclusiveness, and equal rights. It wanted to turn back the clock to a time when strong rulers did what was best for the country and did not tolerate dissent. Elections were suspended, trade unions were banned, and Communists and dissidents were killed or imprisoned. Nazi policies discriminating against Jews and denying their civil rights were vigorously implemented, with the support and help of many ordinary French citizens. According to John Ardagh, "Anti-Semitism became state policy, and deportations of perhaps as many as 150,000 people were organized with an alacrity that haunts France half a century later."[22]

Collaboration between French citizens and Germans was common. Many French helped the Germans by working in their offices, entertaining them in their clubs, or, in the case of many young women, dating German soldiers. For some this was simply a way to survive a bad time, but many French genuinely felt that Hitler's policies would in the end save Europe both from communism and other perceived threats symbolized by the Jews and other "outsiders."

On the other extreme, many French defied the Germans, forming an alliance known as the Résistance. Acts of resistance included traveling miles by foot to deliver important intelligence messages, blowing up bridges, infiltrating the

CHARLES DE GAULLE AND THE FRENCH RÉSISTANCE

Out of one of the most shameful periods of French history sprang one of its great sources of pride, the French Résistance. The movement's center was a French general, Charles de Gaulle, who had escaped to England rather than surrender to the Germans. Once in England he sent radio broadcasts urging the French to resist, and established himself as the international spokesperson for the Résistance.

After the Allied landings at Omaha Beach and other sites in Normandy led to the defeat of Germany and the end of the European part of World War II, Charles de Gaulle was part of the triumphal march up the same stretch of the Champs-Élysées along which the Germans had marched to begin their occupation a few years before. His presence there was a clear indication that the Résistance was considered as much of a fighting force as any army unit had been.

De Gaulle's leadership of the Résistance was more inspirational than practical. He worked outside of France, influencing world leaders and public opinion, while others inside France carried out subversive activities. In fact the Résistance was successful because it did not rely on only a few leaders but on all its members, who were able to work independently within a loosely organized network. Still, no one else in the Résistance came close to his fame and stature (including physical stature: six feet four inches, he towered over all other world leaders), and when France recognized its need for a strong leader in the postwar era, Charles de Gaulle was clearly it. Throughout his presidency, his name and picture remained synonymous with the French people's faith in themselves as a whole.

government, participating in secret transit networks for soldiers trapped behind enemy lines, and hiding dissidents wanted by the Vichy government. People did these things at great risk, knowing they faced death if caught. The risk was highlighted in 1943 when one of the great leaders of the French Résistance, Jean Moulin, was tortured to death by Klaus Barbie, the infamous "Butcher of Lyon." Despite such setbacks, the Résistance continued to play a major role in keeping French hopes alive.

POSTWAR FRANCE

When the war finally ended, the Fourth Republic was declared, but political divisions remained intense. In Paris a dizzying twenty-four governments came and went in only thirteen years. In cities and towns all across France, the social fabric was further torn by a period of vengeance against those accused of collaboration. As many as ten thousand people were executed by vigilantes, and thousands of others were publicly shamed. Women accused of granting sexual favors to Germans, for example, were shaved bald and paraded (sometimes naked) through jeering crowds in the streets.

THE DE GAULLE YEARS

Disunity and distractions at home made France inattentive to its colonies, and in 1954 it lost its hold on what was called French Indochina, when North Vietnam fell to the Communist Vietminh forces at Dien Bien Phu. Independence movements in other colonies such as those in Morocco and Tunisia were growing in strength as well. The hot spot of the French colonial empire, however, was Algeria, where "a savage, dirty war evolved"[23] as a result of deep differences between

Charles de Gaulle gained worldwide respect as a political leader when he ended the Algerian crisis in 1962.

TROUBLE IN ALGERIA

In the decade following the end of World War II, while France struggled to rebuild, its colonies in Africa and Asia mounted bids for independence. In some cases, such as in Morocco, independence was negotiated rather than warred over, but in other countries the issues were so complex and opinions so divided that peaceful solutions proved impossible. This was particularly true in Algeria, which had been a French colony since 1830 and which counted 1 million ethnic French among its 9 million total residents. Those identifying as French were unwilling to simply turn over to ethnic Algerians a country they considered their home, and over time the two groups had fallen into a pattern of increasingly violent confrontations, which spilled over into France itself with terrorist bombings by Algerian independence groups such as the FLN (National Liberation Front).

The French government was powerless to control the escalating violence because it could reach no consensus about what the best solution would be. French colonists took the situation into their own hands by seizing power in Algiers, the capital, in 1958. It appeared that a civil war was inevitable at the time Charles de Gaulle was elected president of France. His role as Résistance leader had gained him a large following across the political spectrum, and he managed to use his popularity to fashion a gradual, orderly withdrawal from Algeria, completed in 1962. This withdrawal included the return to France of well over a million ethnic French from Algeria, as well as from Morocco and Tunisia, a group that became known as the "pieds-noirs," or "black feet," a derogatory term.

ethnic Algerians and French colonists, many of whose families had lived in the North African colony for generations.

Charles de Gaulle, who had become famous as the leader of the Résistance, withdrew into private life after the war, sensing that his time for national leadership had not yet arrived. In 1958, as the Algerian crisis deepened, he was urged to run for president by a broad spectrum of politicians who believed his role in the Résistance would enable him to command the respect of all sides. After his election, de Gaulle was indeed successful in bringing the crisis to an end, structuring a gradual turnover of power, which resulted in full independence for Algeria in 1962. This gained him worldwide respect as a leader, but political and social divisions remained deep at home.

The French economy revived considerably in the 1960s, and the French middle class enjoyed more creature comforts than ever—good housing, vacations, cars, and televisions. Measures taken by the Gaullists (as the de Gaulle government was known) kept inflation in check and increased French profits from international trade. However, these moves increased the gap between haves and have-nots. Taxes increased, wages were frozen, and pensions and subsidies were reduced. Superficially life looked prosperous in France, but underneath, many were still suffering economically, a situation that continues into the present day.

De Gaulle's most lasting legacy is perhaps his most controversial. Determined to reestablish France's national honor after its disgrace in World War II, de Gaulle decided that France would take a leading role in world affairs rather than take a backseat to anyone. Defying American and British foreign policy, de Gaulle sided with Arab countries against Israel, courted friendships with the Soviet Union and China, and deliberately chose to nurture relationships with West Germany over those with Great Britain. He demanded that North Atlantic Treaty Organization (NATO) forces be removed from French soil and developed a French strike force of nuclear weapons. That France would clearly go its own way and follow its own interests was seen by the United States and Great Britain as insulting and ungrateful, coming on the heels of their liberation of France from German control just a few years before. France's relationships with its former allies suffered, but French national pride was unquestionably restored by these actions.

FRANCE SINCE DE GAULLE

De Gaulle seemed invincible in the 1960s. France had been restored to an important international role, and its middle class was living better than ever. Once again, though, events proved surprising. In 1968 the country was rocked by student protest movements focusing on a wide range of French social and economic problems. Workers' groups soon allied with the students, lobbing grenades from behind hastily erected street barricades, similar to those of the Commune in the previous century. When police responded by beating

protesters with clubs in front of television cameras, the situation became a national crisis. For the first time in his political life, de Gaulle was not up to the task of leadership and, rather than try to resolve the situation, he voluntarily resigned from the presidency in 1969.

Parisian students gained national attention in 1968 after their protests erupted into riots.

He was succeeded by Georges Pompidou, a conservative who carried on most of de Gaulle's policies until his death from cancer in 1974. He was succeeded by Valéry Giscard d'Estaing, whose youthful good looks and aristocratic charm gave him a large measure of support, which he used to pass important tax reforms and other measures before he saw his popularity evaporate in the oil crises and economic recessions of the late 1970s. In 1981, the longtime leader of the French Socialists, François Mitterand, became president.

French liberals were excited by the prospect of finally having a president sympathetic to their views. Surely now, they reasoned, such pressing issues as poverty and bad working conditions would be addressed. Mitterand increased wages and pensions, expanded workers' and immigrants' rights, abolished the death penalty, brought some key industries under government control, and gave back many powers to regional and local governments. But Mitterand went too far for some, and a backlash from conservatives gained strength when Mitterand's policies failed to revive the nation's economy. Jean-Marie Le Pen, for example, formed the National Front (*Front National* in French), a racist group that focused on blaming immigrants, particularly dark-skinned ones, for all of France's economic and political turmoil. Le Pen and others never came close to taking power, but were important enough to force Mitterand into many compromises, including naming Jacques Chirac, a conservative and longtime mayor of Paris, as premier in 1986. Chirac eventually defeated Mitterand for the presidency in 1995.

Mitterand was able to hold on to power for fourteen years, longer than any president in French history, and historians generally agree that he is second in importance only to de Gaulle in his role in twentieth-century French history. An intellectual by temperament, Mitterand chose so many teachers for key posts that his government earned the nickname of the "republic of professors."[24] This base enabled him to consider many perspectives before acting, and to anticipate and survive swings in national mood and political challenges from both extremes. His ability to gain support across party lines and to fashion agreements among adversaries was a hallmark of his time in office.

Conservative French president Jacques Chirac faces the challenge of working with a left-wing legislature.

JACQUES CHIRAC

Mitterand was a left-wing president forced to deal with a conservative majority in the legislature. In a country that has always been "a patchwork of polarized groups and political swings,"[25] Jacques Chirac today faces a similar situation; he is a conservative dealing with a left-wing legislature, led by Prime Minister Lionel Jospin, believed by many to be the likely next president of France. Like Mitterand, Chirac's success and political survival will depend on how well he can bring competing interests into agreement, and to a significant degree on how much blame he can avoid for not solving complex problems that are beyond his control. A mix of good fortune and the ability to keep people optimistic and productive seems to make more of a difference in French politics than any specific political orientation or policy. Clearly, if there is one constant in France's history, it is the element of surprise, and Chirac's place in this history is still uncertain.

5

Work, Leisure, and Family Life

The French invented the phrase *joie de vivre* (joy of living), and nowhere is this more evident than in the approach they take to daily life. Whatever the French do in the course of the day, whether work or play, it is infused with the belief that quality of life matters.

The French Home

The foundation of any culture is home life, and the French home reveals much about the French people. Acute housing shortages after World War II led to massive building projects, with the result that more than half the housing today has been built since 1945. The typical middle-class French home is small, whether a freestanding building in a town or suburb, or an apartment in a city. Hasty construction and haphazard remodeling have contributed to general disrepair in much of the housing today, but for people surrounded as the French are with very old buildings and reminders of the primitive ways people used to live, a little peeling paint or water staining seems insignificant.

Most people, rich and poor alike, live in far better conditions than previous generations. Not too long ago it was rare to have a telephone, and many apartments did not have private bathroom facilities. Today it is still rare to find more than one bathroom even in a fairly large home. Closets and other built-in storage are minimal, and bathtubs rather than showers are still the norm, but telephones (most equipped with a computerized telephone directory known as a Minitel) are taken for granted. Homes are furnished in a wide range of ways, but typically furniture is kept for many years, or even generations, and the emphasis is on the home as a family refuge rather than as a fashion statement. In fact, many French prefer socializing with their friends in restaurants rather than having dinner guests in their homes. This is because the home is seen as private and designed only for the family.

FAMILY STRUCTURE AND OBLIGATIONS

The family is by far the most important single aspect of French life. In fact, children are not considered to be adults at a certain age, but only when they have had a child of their own. Families tend to be small, with a national average of less than two children per couple, but extended families are important, and Sunday dinner together, often at grandmother's house, is close to obligatory in many French families.

Each generation has a specific role. Parents are loving disciplinarians who see their role as molding their offspring, not being their playmates. Their main obligation is to provide a good home and a good education for their children. Children are expected to respect all adults, not just their parents. They are also expected to be resourceful in solving their own problems with each other, rather than bothering adults with their squabbles. A child who does not behave well will be severely reprimanded, as a child's manners are seen as a direct reflection on the family. These reprimands do not necessarily come from their own parents; a typical street scene in France is an adult stranger taking to task a young person who has not held open the door or given way on the sidewalk.

This run-down residential building in France is typical of much of the hastily constructed housing built after World War II.

Parent-child obligations remain strong throughout life. As parents grow older, their adult children feel a very strong obligation to meet their parents' physical and financial needs. Generally the goal is to keep parents living independently for as long as possible, and as a result adult children divide the housekeeping, shopping, chauffeuring, nursing, and companionship duties required to allow their parents to continue living in familiar surroundings. Just as the parents helped their newly married children buy and furnish a home years before, the children now are expected to stretch their budgets to meet their parents' additional needs.

THE FRENCH LANGUAGE

Although it is rare to find a French-born person who does not speak French fluently, regional identities are still strong, particularly in Brittany and the Midi, the south of France. This is reflected in the continued survival of their native languages, all as different from French as Italian or Spanish is. In much of rural France, languages such as Breton or Provençal are still part of daily life.

As late as the mid-1500s, there was still no unifying language for the country. Hardly anyone beyond the Île-de-France spoke French. Latin was the language of the church and of government business, and people in the streets and at home spoke a regional tongue. Those who moved beyond their region could not understand people in other parts of France. In 1539, French was declared the official language of the country, and though most published writing from then on was in French, spoken language followed another path. People continued to speak regional languages and learned French only if they discovered they needed to know it. Most did not.

According to John Ardagh and Colin Jones, in *Cultural Atlas of France*, "French remained a minority tongue till 1789," the year of the French Revolution. To address this, public schools began allowing only French, but recently, with a resurgence in regional movements, including weak but quite vocal independence movements in Brittany and Corsica, there is talk of allowing more bilingual instruction and examinations in public schools. To most French this is a step backward, and the issue does not have widespread support, even within the regions affected by it.

EATING, FRENCH STYLE

One of the main budget items of the French family is food. The French are famous worldwide for their cuisine (the French word for cooking), and the typical French person eats very well indeed, whether at home or at a restaurant or café. Although American fast food is quite popular among young people in particular, the French still think of meals as an important part of the day, and they do not think food consumed in five or ten minutes qualifies as a meal. Lunch used to be a two-hour affair, complete with several courses, wine, and good conversation, and though many working people cannot afford to take so much time on a routine basis, a leisurely lunch is still considered the perfect way to break up the day. Many schools take a long enough midday break for children to go home for a good meal, although increasingly children spend the time in day care because the parents cannot be absent from their jobs long enough to pick up their children for the meal and then return them to school.

Dinner is still a family affair, with an emphasis on traditional French dishes and preparations. Though simpler than in former times when food preparation was the major focus of a homemaker's day, dinner still usually consists of more than one course, and the cook pays attention to coordinating the flavors of the meal. It might consist of a simple appetizer, followed by a simply prepared meat, poultry, or fish dish. It might conclude with fruit or cheese, or perhaps a pastry, although the French are not particularly fond of sweet desserts. Soup or salad provide variety from time to time, as do ready-made delicacies of very high quality from neighborhood shops. Dinner is usually eaten fairly late by American standards—usually no earlier than eight—as a result of later quitting times necessitated by the long lunch break. Typically women take responsibility for all aspects of meal preparation, although cooking in and of itself is not considered only women's work—as evidenced by the dominance of men in the ranks of professional chefs.

For eating out, the small neighborhood bistro is a French institution. Family owned and operated, the bistro generally has a limited menu that changes daily depending on what looks good at the morning market. The atmosphere is friendly, often enhanced by inexpensive wine served in clay pitchers. A neighborhood bistro is a good place to catch up on the news, and typically one or more tables are reserved for regulars.

The French still place value on traditional family meals.

365 KINDS OF CHEESE

President Charles de Gaulle once commented on the difficulty of his job by observing that it was not easy to lead any country that had 365 kinds of cheese. To him, the cheeses of France (the number 365 standing for a different one each day of the year, rather than an actual number) symbolized the widely varying styles and preferences of the French people, as well as their belief that their own, of the many possible ways of doing things, is the best. Lovers of French food do not share de Gaulle's purported chagrin, for French cheeses in all their wonderful variety are one of the major gastronomic delights of a country famous for great food.

Perhaps the best-known French cheese is Roquefort, produced in caves from sheep's milk to which a specific mold has been introduced to give it its characteristic blue veins and strong flavor. Other famous French cheeses are Brie and Camembert, but every region has equally wonderful, if less internationally known, varieties. Most are named for the place they are produced, whether it is a town, a valley, or some other location. The cheeses are distinguished from one another by flavor, color, odor, and texture, all of which are the result of the kind and proportion of milk or cream used (cow, sheep, or goat), and the length of aging (from freshly made to aged several years). Additional steps such as washing the rind at specific intervals with a liquid such as beer, salt water, or brandy, or wrapping the cheese in leaves or another substance also contribute to the distinct qualities of the finished products. The French enjoy cheese as a separate course just before dessert or in place of it, and it is also popular as a picnic food or snack.

France is famous for its many varieties of cheese.

Also typical of France is the bar. Each has its usual clients; where people take their coffee is a reflection of their social standing and alliances in the community. A bar will have a few inside tables, but the custom is to stand up while having an espresso, usually sweetened with sugar and tossed down in one gulp (the French do not drink regular coffee or use milk except at breakfast). Some people order a *pression*, or draft beer, at these bars, but hard liquor is rarely consumed. Not only is alcohol very heavily taxed and thus extremely expensive, but also public inebriation is frowned on in France. A bar is not seen as a place to get drunk, but simply to stop for quick refreshment and a bit of conversation during the day. Wine is rarely ordered at bars, because even though the French drink a great deal of wine, it is usually consumed with meals.

EDUCATION

Typically a student in elementary or high school will attend school from around 8:30 to noon, have a substantial lunch break, and then go back to school until around 5:00 P.M. Some schools have classes on Saturday morning, some give students one afternoon off, and some have shortened lunch hours to allow for earlier release time—variations brought about mostly by parental pressure to have their children's schedules better match their own. After a long school day, children have about two hours of homework each night, although the amount has decreased in recent years. Most middle-class French teens do not work, so their after-school time is divided between socializing with their friends and schoolwork.

How much and what kind of homework a student has depends greatly on what kind of academic program the student is taking. Students in France may enroll in either public or private schools; the latter are usually run by the Catholic Church. Both public and private schools receive state funding. Many students in both kinds of schools focus on preparation for specific trades, and the rest prepare for university admission. The most ambitious focus on gaining acceptance at one of the major institutions, Grandes Écoles, which are so prestigious that admission there almost guarantees a future of privilege and wealth.

A MORNING ON BOULEVARD MENILMONTANT

The Boulevard Menilmontant is the center of the twentieth arrondisse-
ment in Paris, which *Insight Guide: France* called "a lively area of off-beat art galleries,
shops, and cafes." Boulevard Menilmontant is particularly notable, however, because it
is here the diversity of Paris can be most fully appreciated. The central strip of the
boulevard is home to an open market, and the shops along either side of the street are
primarily ethnic bakeries, butchers, fruit sellers, and grocers. On one end of Boulevard
Menilmontant, Arabs and North Africans predominate. Swirling music blares from
kiosks selling CDs, while others sell rugs, clothing, and produce. Merchants, mostly
young men, aggressively hawk their tomatoes, spices, and other products to passersby,
who seem indifferent to the chaos. In the bars and cafés lining the street, Middle Eastern men survey the scene and conduct their own business, occasionally puffing on
large water-cooled pipes called hookahs.

Within a few blocks, the clientele and merchants are predominantly Jewish. On Fri-
day morning the scene is particularly lively as Jews prepare for the Sabbath. Trucks pull
up in front of kosher butchers, and men hoist whole hindquarters of beef onto their
shoulders and carry them inside. Bakers advertise their compliance with Jewish dietary
laws on the signs outside their stores, and indicate the particular region, such as Poland
or North Africa, from which their specialties come. Because the Boulevard Menilmontant is a residential neighborhood, other activities go on as well on a typical morning. Here, a man in a yarmulke, the small skullcap that many Jews wear, takes his two
small children, also wearing yarmulkes and carrying backpacks, to school. There, a
young Algerian man rushes home with a bag of pastries for his family. The Boulevard
Menilmontant serves as a reminder that Paris, like France itself, is a multiethnic society,
a melting pot.

Overall, however, in today's France the perception is that
schools have declined in their ability to reward students with
a reasonable chance for success in their chosen field, or provide students with a good background in French culture.
Baccalauréat programs (similar to the American high school
diploma) often seem filled with unnecessary busywork, and
a strong emphasis on math and science in all programs has
detracted from studies in art, literature, and history—areas
in which the French contribution has been particularly
strong. Therefore, though providing a good education for
one's children is considered one of the hallmarks of good
parenting in France, and though school continues to be the
center of children's social lives, education is no longer
treated with quite the awe and reverence enjoyed only a few
generations ago when schooling first became compulsory.

THE WORLD OF WORK

Despite the lack of enthusiasm of some for school, it is clear, in the words of author Theodore Zeldin, that "what keeps France [going] is that the majority are firmly attached to the belief that by hard work it is possible to succeed in life."[26] As in any other modern nation, generalizations about work are difficult because jobs and workplaces vary so much, but the French do share the attitude that work is an important element of human dignity and worth. In fact, even the richest French serve as heads of corporations, run for political office, or do philanthropic work, stressing their work over their family name, and certainly over the size of their fortune, which is always downplayed as a matter of good taste.

One in four employees in France works for the government in some capacity or another, whether as a government minister, file clerk, municipal police officer, or teacher. This amounts to a huge bureaucracy, much larger than that in the United States. This tendency began in the time of Napoléon, who introduced a legal and administrative system that got the government involved in regulating a wide range of things relating to business, the law, and personal life that people had previously handled among themselves. Now what characterizes business and other transactions in France is a mountain of paperwork, the handling of which requires many steps and approvals, each requiring a different person. This is inefficient and annoying, and has produced what the French call "le Système D," a term for the way one must go around the rules and procedures to *débrouiller*, or untangle, situations in order to get anything done.

Young students complete a school assignment on an outdoor stairway in Paris.

But bureaucratic tangles, annoying as they are for those who must stand in long lines or wait months for something in the mail, do make work for many, and thus provide job security, which some foreign observers regard as the essential concern of the French office worker. Though many wish to become bosses or middle managers, lacking ambition is not seen as laziness. Work at any level is seen as dignified, but primarily a means of providing for a family, rather than as a source of personal fulfillment and gratification.

The emphasis on simply having and keeping an adequately paid job is reflected in the pace and practices of the workplace. One is expected to work steadily, but not to hurry. Work is not a competition, and the more flexible and cooperative one is, the better. French workplaces are governed by important unwritten rules of politeness, which include much handshaking, much formality in addressing each other regardless of rank, and much stopping to chat with coworkers, clients, and customers. Even at a long business lunch, it would be impolite to mention business at all until after the main dish has been cleared. In these and other ways, the French respect the dignity and complexity of each person with whom they interact.

RELAXING, FRENCH STYLE

Balancing work and leisure are of paramount concern to the French, as indicated by the fact that labor reforms have stressed such things as establishing a standard forty-hour workweek (recently reduced to thirty-five) and five weeks of paid vacation a year. Work and "real life" are totally separate, and in fact it is considered poor manners to ask a French per-

During their leisure time, many Parisians enjoy strolling the streets and stopping at local cafés.

son what he or she does for a living. Showing any interest at all in how much money a person makes, according to writer Sally Adamson Taylor, is even worse, for the French "find the subject of money indecent."[27] Far more interesting is finding out what people's political views are, what they think of the meal they are eating, or what their children are up to. This insistence on working to live, not living to work, creates a culture that even today emphasizes enjoyment of the little things in life, such as stopping in a café in the middle of running errands, buying dinner ingredients daily if possible, and relaxing at home or with friends in the evening.

Though many French also enjoy structured leisure time such as that provided by team sports, for the most part they prefer their leisure time to be light on commitments. They prefer spur of the moment activities, and go to the movies far more often than other Europeans do. The French have also joined the fitness craze. "Le jogging" is a popular activity, and many swimming and gym facilities have sprung up in recent years. Nice weather on a Saturday will send many city families out to the countryside for a drive and a nice lunch, or send suburbanites into the city for shopping. Though France is 90 percent Catholic, church is not a part of the typical French person's week, although most celebrate Christmas extravagantly and appreciate the days off provided by religious holidays. Important annual sporting events such as the Tour de France and the French Open, and some regional and seasonal activities such as bullfighting in the south and skiing in the Alps, draw huge crowds, but French leisure is more characterized by walks in the park, shopping, a quick visit to a museum, a morning of tennis, time in a comfortable chair with a favorite magazine, or doing nothing at all.

GOING ON VACATION

Those who can get away for more than a day or two tend to favor two particular kinds of holidays. The first is "le camping," which has surged in popularity in recent years as a result of the fitness craze. Whether backpacking in the remote regions of the Pyrenees, fly-fishing in the Ardèche, or enjoying a more luxurious and structured campground along the Mediterranean coast, over 5 million French, up from 1 million in 1950, now make camping one of the nation's top vacation choices.

THE TOUR DE FRANCE

The Tour de France is unquestionably the most famous and important bicycle race in the world. It has had different beginning points over the years and different overall lengths, but the race, which stretches over several weeks each July, makes a circle through France, ending each year with a sprint down the Champs-Élysées in Paris, to the applause of huge crowds in the bleachers erected for the occasion.

The first Tour was held in 1903 as an advertising gimmick. The bicycles had only a single gear and balloon tires, and the riders were amateurs. In one early Tour, a competitor whose bike had broken had to run nine miles carrying the bike over his shoulder to a village where he could get it repaired. Today, trained staff accompanies the riders, and camera crews and support services follow along in specially equipped trucks. Crowds line the route, which covers some of the most spectacular scenery in France.

The riders today are professionals, all men, usually part of a team whose overall strategy is to create the most favorable conditions for their lead member, such as setting a pace they know they cannot keep, in order to tire out another favorite. Unfortunately, because the speed of bicycling exposes the body to great harm from falls, there have been serious and even fatal accidents over the years, but this has not deterred the growth of the competition. Although the goal is to win the Tour de France altogether, the race is kept interesting each day by daily prizes for the best time, awards to the best rookies, and special competitions for particular terrains such as mountain passes. Though French and Belgian cyclists have dominated the race historically, recent winners have included Americans such as Greg Lemond and Lance Armstrong, whose comeback after chemotherapy for cancer to win in 1999, 2000, and 2001 inspired many around the world.

Cyclists make their way through the French Alps during the Tour de France.

A second type of vacation, the resort village, is also prized by the French. The world famous Club Med was invented in France (although by a Belgian, Gerard Blitz) in 1950, and has grown from "little groups of straw huts by beaches"[28] to approximately one hundred luxurious resorts worldwide and dozens more imitators of its all-inclusive format. Though also extremely popular with Americans, 40 percent of the vacationers are still French. The French particularly like Club Med because it caters to their tastes and sensitivities. No money is exchanged. Excellent food and wine are included in the price of the vacation, and individual purchases are made with plastic beads that have been discreetly purchased upon arrival at the camp. The classic French formality is set aside for the week, with campers encouraged to address one another as "tu," the intimate pronoun normally reserved for family and close friends.

The French have traditionally taken vacations in late July or August. This custom is so strong that campgrounds and resort villages are packed at that time and populated the rest of the year only by Americans and other foreigners who plan vacations for the off-season. It used to be said that one could not meet a Parisian in Paris in August, because "the true Parisian is . . . to be found somewhere on a beach, along with all the other Parisians."[29] Though the government has tried to provide incentives to have people stagger their vacations, such as offering longer school holidays at other times of the year, the custom still holds. Until recently, the French generally tended to vacation in France, but in recent years the crowding of French resort villages and towns such as Antibes and Cannes on the Riviera has been reduced somewhat by a new French interest in traveling abroad, but not usually farther than Italy, Spain, or Greece.

"C'EST LA VIE"

The French are not immune from the stresses of everyday life. Often, having too much to do prevents the enjoyment of other aspects of life. Work and school create stresses. Family crises afflict the French as often as anyone else. Money, though not spoken of as important, is a constant worry for the poor and for the middle class as well, who struggle to provide a better future for their children than they had. Births, marriages, and deaths punctuate every year, and the

THE MINITEL

Next to the telephone in the typical French home is a small screen and keyboard known as a Minitel, an electronic telephone directory linked also to newspapers, booking offices, mail-order services, and on-line dating networks, as well as to reference materials such as encyclopedias. The French are rightly proud of this sign of their creativity and versatility in the modern era, for the Minitel was in place in 1984, long before the Internet became a fixture in American lives. France Telecom, the national phone service, originally pioneered the idea as a way of getting rid of cumbersome phone directories, and the first Minitels were offered free of charge to everyone with a phone. However, its other uses became quickly apparent, and today those who wish to use more than the basic service pay a small fee. Today 6.5 million phones are equipped with Minitels, 80 percent of them in private residences.

Being on the cutting edge can have its drawbacks, however, and the efficiency and thoroughness of the Minitel system have hampered enthusiasm for the Internet. Because the Minitel does not require a computer or a modem, schools and even many businesses have not invested in the hardware and software that would make them part of the "information highway." Only about a half-million French businesses and homes have Internet access, compared with over 40 million in the United States. This means that only 16 percent of French homes have a personal computer, and even many schools do not have a single one. Purchases are skyrocketing, however, and the Minitel, it is expected, will fade in importance as the French are lured into cyberspace.

changes these bring about increase anxieties and pressures. However, the French seem more capable than most of shrugging off the stress with an expression known worldwide, *"C'est la vie"* ("That's life"), then turning their attention to the small pleasure of drinking a cup of espresso, or picking cherries one by one at a fruit stand, or stopping to browse at a bookstall along the Seine. It is no wonder that the French have a reputation for knowing how to live, for they practice it every day.

Subtlety and Surprise: Arts and Culture in France

In Brittany, a woman bends over an intricate array of pins and bobbins as her deft fingers loop and knot fine, white threads into delicate lace to adorn the collar of a blouse. In Provence, textile mills churn out miles of printed fabric with colors as bright as the poppies, lavender, and sunflowers in the surrounding fields, to be turned into scarves, tablecloths, or curtains. In Lyon, buyers from the fashion houses of Paris pore over bolts of thick, subtly colored silk brocade in small wholesalers' shops, looking for just the right fabric for a jacket for one of the world's richest women. These three isolated activities demonstrate one of the essential elements of French culture—a belief that delight of the senses is one of the main pleasures of life.

French taste, whether in food, fashion, or the arts, is characterized by a few common elements. The first of these is subtlety. French food, for example, is prepared in a way that either showcases one ingredient's essential qualities or creates a delicate combination of flavors that makes the diner want each bite to last a lifetime. A French cook might spend hours preparing stuffing for a whole chicken from which he or she had deftly managed to remove all the bones, then might labor over a sauce to pour over the dish at the table. Every ingredient will be carefully thought out for the proper balance of flavors, textures, and visual appearance. Alongside this masterpiece the cook may serve a simple vegetable, picked within hours of dining and complemented only with butter that is equally fresh.

A second quality common to French taste is the element of surprise. Chefs routinely experiment with the physical appearance of food on the plate to add this element of surprise. A piece of fish may perch atop a carefully constructed pyramid of brightly colored vegetables, or a scoop of ice cream may be garnished with three different carefully drizzled sauces, forming a pattern worthy of a modern art gallery. The diners will appreciate all aspects of this delightful meal—both its simple perfections and its artistry—because separately and together all these elements enhance their awareness and appreciation of the experience of eating good food. This, in turn, enhances their awareness and appreciation of being alive.

FASHION

Awareness and appreciation of life through attention to subtle details and little surprises is at the core of one of the most famous of French art forms, haute couture, or "high fashion." Though France had been the center of fashion for centuries, it reached its modern heights after World War II, with fashion designers such as Dior, St. Laurent, Cardin, and Chanel. Despite now having to share their fame with Americans such as Calvin Klein and Italians such as Giorgio Armani, these French designers are still household words

A model poses on the runway at a Paris fashion show.

today. At the core of high fashion are the fabrics from which the clothing is made, and it is here that the French love of subtlety comes into play. The fabrics are exquisitely made, beautiful to look at, and wonderful to feel even before they are cut. The cuts for the clothing are meticulous and designed to accent both the quality of the fabric and the body contours of the wearer.

When many think of haute couture, they imagine runway models in unusual hats and bizarre makeup, wearing outlandish clothing. This is part of high fashion as well—making clothing and the presentation of it an art form without concern for such things as whether a person could get in a car, eat a meal, or even sit down while wearing such fashions. It is here that the French love of surprise is indulged to the height, and indeed the creativity of fashion shows does carry over into the typical French woman's fashion sense when she tosses a brightly colored scarf over the shoulder of an otherwise very plain (but well-cut) outfit, or when a man chooses exquisite enameled cuff links to go with his immaculate white shirt. The way the French men and women dress, at least in the cities, clearly conveys the message that daily details such as choosing what to wear are an important element in appreciating life.

THE VISUAL ARTS

Subtlety and surprise are hallmarks of French painting, sculpture, and architecture as well. The medieval Bayeux Tapestry, a 120-foot-long weaving that depicts the story of William of Normandy's conquest of England, still astonishes today with its details. Later, in the seventeenth century, Claude Lorrain (1600–1682) painted large landscapes famous for their dramatic use of light and painstaking detail. In subsequent generations, painters such as Antoine Watteau (1684–1721) and Jean-Honoré Fragonard (1732–1806) depicted the frivolous life of the royal court in delicately colored paintings in which every lace cuff and every leaf on a tree is given due attention. Among the most famous of these is Fragonard's *The Swing*, which depicts a sumptuously dressed young woman losing a dainty slipper as she swings in a wooded garden, while two mysterious figures watch from the shadows. Painting in a very different style, Jacques-Louis David (1748–1825) and J.A.D. Ingres (1780–1867) are renowned for their remarkable ability to paint human skin and fabrics with a realism approaching a photograph.

It was in the mid–nineteenth century, with the Impressionists, that French painting reached heights of inventiveness unsurpassed before or since. The Impressionists focused on a different kind of reality, the dazzle of light and color on the eye, rather than the small, easily overlooked details, which were the focus of previous generations of painters. The Impressionists were so named because of the scoffing comment made by one early critic, that their paintings were scarcely more than impressions, not finished works. The Impressionists were the first to work out of doors, a development made possible by the invention of tube paint. Some painters, most notably Claude Monet (1840–1926), took advantage of this to paint the same scene many times in different seasons and times of day. Some of his most famous paintings are of a water lily garden at Giverny, his home out-

The medieval Bayeux Tapestry depicts the Norman conquest of England in 1066.

ASTERIX AND OBELIX

One of the most popular cartoon characters around the world is Asterix, as much a part of French culture as baguettes (long, thin loaves of bread), Minitels, and espresso. The setting is Roman Gaul around 50 B.C., where in a small town in today's Brittany a short blond man with a big nose sets off to solve the problems the Roman occupation causes the villagers. He is accompanied by a huge friend, Obelix, a deliveryman often seen carrying huge stone menhirs on his back, who always proposes a good meal as the answer to all problems. Asterix is aided in his superhuman feats by a Druid potion made by the local priest, called Getafix in English translations, and by the village chief, Vitalstatistix.

The charm of Asterix is its intelligence. Puns abound in the names of characters, such as Epidemix the fishmonger and his wife, Bacteria. Literary, historical, and contemporary references abound, giving Asterix a reputation as a cartoon for both children and educated and sophisticated adults alike. Even Asterix's name is a play on the Gallic hero Vercingetorix, but Asterix is simply an asterisk, or footnote, sweetly but clearly deluded in his dreams of glory. According to Theodore Zeldin in *The French*, "After General de Gaulle, Asterix is the best known Frenchman of modern times . . . even if he makes fun of all that Frenchmen are supposed to stand for and worship." More than twenty books of his exploits have been published, each selling over 2 million copies each. Asterix has also been translated into over twenty foreign languages, and it is as popular in Germany as it is in France.

side Paris. The Impressionist style is characterized by broad, quick brush strokes, dots of white and dark paint to suggest light and shadow, and the techniques of "dragging" and "wet on wet," whereby one color of paint is applied on top of another, still-wet color and the blending is done directly on the canvas.

Other famous French Impressionists include Edgar Degas (1834–1917), whose fascination with the newly invented camera caused him to rethink basic ideas of composition in a painting. He gave his paintings a sense of movement and immediacy by cutting off figures at the edges of the canvas to make it look like they were either about to leave or had not totally entered the painting. By these and other techniques, he gave his paintings of ballerinas, horse races, and other subjects a snapshot quality. One other noteworthy nineteenth-century French painter was Paul Cézanne (1839–1906), often called the father of modern painting because of his interest in structuring his paintings around basic colors and shapes. The oranges in his still lifes, for example, are little more than brightly colored discs, and his paintings of landscapes emphasize triangles, rectangles, and other geometric shapes.

After the Impressionists, France produced several more significant painters, including Paul Gauguin, Henri Matisse, and René Magritte, as well as one of the greatest sculptors of the modern era, Auguste Rodin, whose massive compositions *The Thinker* and *The Kiss* are among the most widely recognized in the world. However, it was as a haven for expatriate painters such as Pablo Picasso, who left his native Spain at the beginning of the twentieth century; and Marc Chagall, whose radical and original style, as well as his Jewish faith, forced him from his native Russia, that France

SANTONS

Of the many folk arts surviving today in France, none is more loved than the *santon*. Derived from the word "saint," *santons* originally were figures from the story of Jesus' birth used in nativity scenes in churches. Originating in Marseille, these small painted clay figures soon became part of home celebrations of Christmas. Over time families began to add *santons* far removed from the original story, representing people familiar to them. Butchers, fishermen, parish priests, and others appeared, followed by humorous figures of quarreling children, pesky dogs, young lovers, and other representatives of daily life, all dressed in traditional Provençal clothing. Elaborate three-dimensional settings for huge collections of *santons* arranged to look as if daily life is simply going on while Jesus is being born are set up each year in many Provençal towns as a focal point of the Christmas season.

Today *santons* are mass-produced for sale at Christmas and year-round in tourist centers. Some are cheap in quality and price, but an expertly hand-fashioned and hand-painted *santon* depicting, for example, a group of women laughing on a park bench, or a couple in wedding clothes, now costs hundreds of dollars.

(particularly Paris) made its mark in the twentieth-century art world. Even today, as author John Ardagh remarks, with a few exceptions, "very few post-war French artists have had any wide international impact."[30] The French are still very interested in art—they put on some of the best exhibitions and have some of the finest museums in the world—but their focus is not usually on contemporary French artists.

Music

The French have a long history of achievement and interest in music, although their accomplishments have often been overshadowed by German and Italian composers. Part of the reason for this lies precisely in the characteristics of subtlety and surprise at the heart of French taste. Compared with other music of the nineteenth century, French music strove for effects similar to those of Impressionist painting, playing with sounds as a way of creating a mood, or describing a place or an emotion. Hector Berlioz (1803–1869), one of France's greatest composers, astonished his audience with his *Symphonie fantastique*, in which he developed a story of a young man's dream of love with an unattainable young woman. He pioneered the idea of a theme melody, or idée fixe (fixed idea), to represent the young woman, so that every time even a few of its lush and graceful notes are played, the audience is reminded of the young man's infatuation with her.

Auguste Rodin created the famous sculpture The Thinker.

The music of Berlioz and other major French composers such as Camille Saint-Saëns, Claude Debussy, Gabriel Fauré, and César Franck have received less recognition than some

THE CHANSON

Dating to medieval times, when minstrels used to amuse the lords and ladies at court with songs of love and heroism, the chanson (which means simply "song") is still a vibrant part of French culture in modern times. The term chanson is used for songs that are poetic and very personal, often sung by their composers. They commonly focus on the heartbreak of love—betrayal, abandonment, love lost, and love that never could be. The chanson shows a weariness with the world usually conveyed by a slow tempo and a voice filled with subtle emotion. Perhaps the most famous singer of chansons is Edith Piaf (1915–1963), who was abandoned at birth and lived as a child on the coins she got from singing in the streets of Paris. Eventually someone took an interest in training her voice, and she became a major star with songs such as "Je ne regrette rien" ("I Regret Nothing") and "La Vie en rose" (which translates roughly as "Rose-Colored Life"). Today artists such as Michel LeGrand carry on the tradition of the chanson, with such compositions as "The Wind-mills of My Mind." In the United States, Frank Sinatra adapted the style of the chanson for some of his greatest hits, such as "It Was a Very Good Year."

Edith Piaf gained international fame for her chanson-style songs.

other composers have enjoyed, in part precisely because French music is subtle and requires close attention. Such attention is amply rewarded by the remarkable beauty and inventiveness of the scores. Two French composers, however, stand at the forefront of popularity. Maurice Ravel's *Bolero*, with its hypnotic repeated melody, is one of the best-known symphonic compositions of all time. The opera *Carmen*, by French composer Georges Bizet, is the second most frequently performed opera in the world. Important modern composers are Darius Milhaud, Olivier Messaien, and Pierre Boulez, France's leading conductor and composer. One of Messaien's best-known compositions is *Quartet for the End of Time*, written while he was a prisoner during World War II, using a violin, clarinet, cello, and piano, the only four instruments available in the camp. In his seventies, Boulez is still active, promoting alternative theories and styles of music that remain very much a minority taste.

LITERATURE

Boulez is only one in a long tradition of unconventional artistic figures, such as the poet Gerard de Nerval, who paraded down the Champs-Élysées with his pet lobster, and novelist George Sand, who used a man's name, man's clothing, and man's habits such as smoking as a way of demanding the same social liberties men enjoyed in the nineteenth century. But there is probably no country in the world that has produced as many great mainstream writers of international renown as France. Shelf after library shelf is filled with close to a millennium's worth of great literature. The last three hundred years alone have seen a staggering number of literary giants, including seventeenth-century playwrights Molière, Racine, and Corneille; the eighteenth-century philosophes; nineteenth-century novelists Hugo, Balzac, Flaubert, and Stendhal, and poets Baudelaire, Rimbaud (whose reputation had been established for all time before he quit writing poetry at age nineteen), Mallarmé, and Verlaine; and twentieth-century figures such as Malraux, Desnos, Gide, Camus, Sartre, Beauvoir, and Robbe-Grillet, all famous novelists and essayists. There is no field of intellectual endeavor in which the French

Novelist George Sand caused controversy in France with her unconventional lifestyle.

FRENCH WITH AN ACCENT

American advertisers have long used people's attitudes toward particular accents as a way of marketing products effectively. For many Americans, for example, a French accent is a sign of sophistication, culture, and good taste. Likewise, the French also associate cultural traits with the way their language is spoken. According to journalist Matthew Alice, writing in "Straight from the Hip," an American accent is a must for selling products associated with the United States, such as tortilla chips or jeans. "The perfect American-accented French . . . will have a sort of . . . twang to it," much like the way Texans sound, because "to a Frenchman . . . the definitive American is the cowboy."

The French also have associations with other languages, and view French spoken with a British accent as conveying snobbery or upper-class distinctiveness, and German-accented French as authoritarian and businesslike. But the most important thing to the French is to hear their language spoken well, a difficult task for non-native speakers. Indeed, the feelings of many French toward their language is well captured by British playwright Noel Coward, quoted in *Insight Guide: France*, who, when asked upon Charles de Gaulle's death what he thought God and the general would talk about in heaven, replied, "That depends on how good God's French is."

have not excelled, and their achievements with the written word—philosophy, poetry, drama, and fiction—are unsurpassed. Today when people read or go to see *The Hunchback of Notre Dame, Planet of the Apes, The Three Musketeers, Twenty Thousand Leagues under the Sea, Les Misérables,* or *Phantom of the Opera*, they are enjoying only a small sample of the creative genius of the French.

FILM

For decades the French have had one of the most internationally respected film industries. Since the Lumière brothers invented cinematography in Lyon in 1885, France has been in the forefront, although today, as with the other arts, they seem to be resting on past glories rather than developing the next generation of geniuses. Among famous early directors are Jean Cocteau and Jean Renoir, son of the famous Impressionist painter Pierre-Auguste Renoir. Both of these directors saw how film could be used as an extension of other arts such as poetry and painting to present both fantasies and everyday life in a way that heightened their meaning. *La Belle et la Bête* is Cocteau's dreamlike retelling of the story of Beauty and the Beast, and *La Grande Illusion*, one of Renoir's masterpieces, depicts the tragedy of World War I through enemies thrown together in a prisoner of war camp.

In the 1950s a group of young directors called the New Wave revitalized a film industry feeling the loss of its earlier giants, and in so doing, put France in the forefront of the international market for high-quality films. Such was their clout that the Cannes Film Festival and its prestigious prize, the *paume d'or* (golden palm), soon became synonymous with excellence in film. These directors included Jean-Luc Goddard, whose 1959 film *Au Bout de Souffle* was recently remade in the United States as *Breathless*, starring Richard Gere; and François Truffaut, best known outside France for *Jules et Jim* (1961). Louis Malle, another New Wave director, is unusual in his range, producing American films such as *Pretty Baby* and *Atlantic City;* documentary-style films such as *My Dinner with André* (a full-length film consisting of a dinner conversation between two brilliant men in New York theater); and enduring dramas such as *Au Revoir les Enfants.* This last film is autobiographical and, according to

Prolific director Louis Malle helped revitalize the French film industry.

journalist Louis-Bernard Robitaille, depicts "a cruel episode it would take [Malle] forty years to exorcise"[31]: Malle's boyhood experience in a Catholic boarding school during World War II, where he befriends, and inadvertently betrays to the Nazis, a young Jewish boy being passed off as Catholic.

The element of subtlety and surprise is at the core of what delights audiences about French films. The French coined the term *film d'auteur* to describe a central value of their cinema, that a film should be the director's personal vision, expressing his or her own interests and personality. French films for this reason tend to be fairly low budget and extraordinarily diverse, and for the most part they are quiet, thoughtful affairs, focusing not on big social issues but on everyday life and ordinary people. French filmmakers recognize that this highly personal approach will not draw in mass audiences, and they do not try to do so, nor do most of their films ever screen outside of France. American big-budget imports flood the large theaters, while small movie houses, particularly in Paris, do a good business among the better educated, who provide most of the support for the French film industry.

REVIVAL

Although approximately 130 films are produced each year in France, in recent years, France has seen a decline in the number of high-quality films, just as it has seen a decline in its other art forms. However, a revival of interest in the arts has been apparent since the 1990s, with more and more French showing an interest in attending concerts, opera, ballet, and serious art films. On almost any evening, churches and public rooms resound with vocal, orchestral, or chamber music, to the delight of growing audiences, usually dressed as if they have just come from work. Operas and ballets are frequently sold out, and conservatories have been overwhelmed by the growth in demand for admission to study music, art, and dance.

This growth in interest in the arts crosses class boundaries as well as regions, with parents clamoring across the country for more emphasis on music and other cultural refinements in the schools. Young adults, on their own initiative, are learning how to play musical instruments and even taking up ballet, which has become very chic as a hobby in recent years. This newfound desire to participate in the arts should come as no surprise, because it is in the doing that the subtleties and surprises of any art form are revealed. Through the personal revelation that mastering a clarinet solo or a pas de deux in ballet brings to the doer, the "joie de vivre," the joy of being alive, that is so much a part of the French character, is celebrated and renewed.

7

CONTEMPORARY FRANCE: CHALLENGES AND CHANGES

Until recently French culture has been characterized by tradition and continuity. Although France today still gets much of its identity from past glories and long-standing customs, it has been faced in the last few decades with the realization that neither its history nor its traditional ways of seeing and doing things will be enough to keep the country peaceful and productive as a nation or a vital force on the international stage.

The twentieth century was a period of great insights or, some might argue, shocks for the French people. The country that produced Charlemagne and Napoleon was occupied by Germany in two world wars, requiring rescue by nations it had seen as its cultural inferiors. The country that had produced great humanitarians such as Voltaire and Rousseau was the only European nation to collaborate actively and officially with the Nazis, including their efforts to exterminate Jews. After the war, feelings of national disgrace led many to question whether France was even entitled to a role as a world leader.

Though Charles de Gaulle was able to rekindle a sense of French pride, the post–World War II era was a time of intense self-evaluation. The student protests of 1968, which quickly grew to involve a wider range of people than had ever participated in protests before, raised issues that have not been fully resolved even today. Likewise, the dark side of French pride, the tolerance of intolerance, still stings the national conscience and negatively impacts millions of French citizens. Yet France, according to historians and social scientists alike, seems more ready than ever to tackle its social and other problems, rather than assuming that the nation can continue as it always has, simply because it is France.

THE FRENCH IDENTITY AT HOME

The French are, above all, a nation of worriers when it comes to political, social, and economic matters. They are fond of using the word *crise*, or crisis, to describe troublesome trends, and are often described as possessing *morosité*, or gloomy thinking about the future. One of their main worries today is that the unique French culture is being lost. France is not alone in its concern that the extreme domination of the United States, as the major global commercial power and cultural trendsetter around the world, has had a destructive impact on national cultures. Today in any French city, a

McDonald's restaurants can be found in most French cities. Many French people are concerned that Americanization threatens French culture.

typical shopping street will sport a Starbucks and a McDonald's, as well as other American chain stores. Billboards will promote the latest American films, subtitled or dubbed in French. Even when the product is French, as with much television programming, it is often a clone of American game shows and soap operas.

According to journalist John Ardagh, "French and foreigners alike are aware that much of what is best and best-loved about France . . . is bound up with a certain traditional civilized way of life and thought—in the arts and philosophy, in food, conversation and much else."[32] It is easy to see how a McDonald's packed with young people dressed in Gap T-shirts and Polo jeans, downing lunch in fifteen minutes, and interspersing their chatter with American slang and English terms such as "weekend" and "e-mail" would worry those whose ideas of being French include sitting down for a leisurely meal, patronizing cafés and restaurants owned and operated by locals and serving typical French dishes, and speaking their language without the need to borrow words from others.

Americanization is not the only thing that seems threatening to the French identity. For several generations the Catholic Church, so much a part of the history and culture of France, has suffered a decline. Although regular attendance reaches as high as 75 to 80 percent in some rural villages, it is as low as 4 to 5 percent in Paris. Likewise, the French family, traditionally presided over by a loving but domineering "papa," and run in a very disciplined and structured fashion, has seen recent generations of children simply refuse to accept long-standing rules and expectations for their behavior. At work the same phenomenon holds. People are less willing than before to tolerate limitations on their upward mobility based on their social class or their connections. Additionally, many young people feel they have more in common with other youth around the world than with the French of other generations. Many feel that the French identity has already been significantly lost by these developments.

THE FRENCH IMAGE ABROAD

Today these feelings of loss are heightened by worries about whether France will be in the future an international power of the first magnitude. It was one of the key leaders in the movement to establish a single currency, the Euro, for all Europe, and it has provided much of the creative energy behind the European Union (EU), a multinational agreement to treat all member nations as if they were one country for purposes of trade and travel. Still, fears abound among the French people as to whether these will only be the first official steps in their cultural extinction. The French have a phrase, *"l'exception française"* ("the French exception"), which they use in a half-joking manner to refer to their belief that they are different from others and that generalities simply do not apply to them. Being part of the European Union specifically designed to reduce exceptions in favor of common interests is a worrisome proposition. Gone are the days when President de Gaulle dared to inflame the world by presenting the French as apart (and above) the rest of the world. Now France struggles to hold on to equal economic and political status with neighboring Italy and Germany, and even with England, its greatest traditional rival.

The French have also seen their international reputation as trendsetters fade over the last few decades. In the 1950s, the city synonymous with high fashion was Paris, and the country synonymous with culture was France. Even the vocabulary used in English to describe sophisticated things often was French. For example, the word *cuisine* came to stand for something more than mere cooking, *boutique* became the term for a small (and usually expensive) store, and *couture* became the way to describe clothing that was more than merely the latest arrival at the local shopping center. French wines set the standard for the world, and a familiarity with French films was a sign of great sophistication in the United States and elsewhere.

Today, Milan has eclipsed Paris as the main fashion center of the world. Though Paris is still important, it shares its status with New York and other cities. French cooking is still respected worldwide as one of the world's great cuisines, but most people would be reluctant to place it above all others. And although the great French wines still command astronomical prices, wines from California and other places around the world are equally praised outside of France. The label "Made in France" does not command the immediate respect it once did. Even in education, the Sorbonne in Paris

Although France still produces some of the finest wines in the world, wines from other countries are equally praised.

is now only one of many places to study the arts rather than the foremost place in the world.

THE CHANGING WORKPLACE

Whether such changes constitute a decline, or are simply signs of an increasingly globalized world culture in which France is actually holding its own quite well, is a matter of intense debate. However, it is clear that France is facing many economic challenges impacting its present and future. One example is farming, which traditionally involved individual farmers working without benefit of modern equipment on small farms. Today, except in isolated regions, the peasant farmer is a thing of the past. Farmers are now businesspeople, generally working larger holdings than a few generations ago, using modern machinery, and promoting sales by means of organized cooperatives. On the downside, they must compete with huge agribusinesses with the means to put cutting-edge technology and marketing strategies to their advantage. As a result, the small farmer is better off than in the past but still struggles to compete successfully.

In industry, the French social class structure and reluctance to embrace change have made reforms difficult. Traditionally, businesses were run by aristocrats who had no experience doing the actual labor of their own plants and companies. They saw no need to consult with or even acknowledge the existence of their workers. Even among managers, cooperation was uncommon, as upper management was unwilling to delegate authority or responsibility to those below them. As a result, French businesses were not efficient, and they fell behind their German and British counterparts. Trade unions have never been particularly strong in France, as they tend to be tied to specific political parties and thus

THE NATIONAL SPORT OF TAX EVASION

Social class, though weakening as a barrier to upward mobility, remains a powerful force in the French economy today. Managers typically make seven to eight times the pay of unskilled workers, a much greater difference than in other European countries. The French tax structure provides many breaks to the higher paid, but even so, according to writer John Ardagh, income tax evasion by highly paid professionals "is a very rewarding old French pastime." A lawyer in private practice, for example, will declare only a small portion of his or her income, and the tax inspectors will generally not question it. Those employed by the state (over one-quarter of the working population) cannot do this so easily. As a result of the difficulty in getting the wealthiest French to pay taxes, France has relied on the value-added tax system (VAT). Under this system, large purchases and purchases of luxury goods are taxed at the time of purchase, similar to a sales tax. The theory is that those who have the money to buy more than they actually need will, in this fashion, pay the additional taxes they probably are avoiding. The problem, of course, is that a poor person who has saved for a car for years will pay the same value-added tax as someone for whom the car is a minor purchase. So far the French governments of socialists and conservatives alike have failed to figure out how to address the discrepancies in the French tax system.

cannot muster the loyalty of all workers. Employee associations are still a rarity, existing primarily to sponsor the occasional company party and offering little else to their members. This is slowly changing as French businesses try out Japanese and American techniques of consultative management, incentives for employee creativity and productivity, less secrecy about management of the company, and support for employee organizations that promote job loyalty and connectedness among workers.

A CLOGGED BUREAUCRACY

Change in the normal way of doing business has come even more slowly to the government than to industry. France has the most cumbersome and inefficient bureaucracy in Europe. Almost every aspect of business requires governmental permission, approval, oversight, planning, and implementation. Education, the police and justice systems, medical care, welfare, public utilities, and many aspects of finance and local government all cannot function except at the pace set by the central government offices to which they report. Many French understand that to remain competitive in the new global economy, far more emphasis must be placed on allowing businesses to do what they do best—make a profit—and this will require giving them more room to function without so much government interference. Less time is spent filling out paperwork and observing countless meaningless procedures than a decade ago, but bureaucracy is still a major deterrent to doing business in France. Even on the individual level there has been some relief. In Bordeaux, for example, the time required to renew a driver's license has been cut from three weeks to three hours.

SOCIAL SERVICES AND EDUCATION

The relationship of the French people to their government is a complex one, because much as they despise the bureaucracy, they, more than any other Western European nation, demand that the government step in to meet their needs. For example, if a school needs new front doors, the parents and teachers would be more likely to lead a demonstration to demand new doors than figure out a way to raise the funds themselves. For years parents have routinely received government money for each of their children, to help with the

LE SYSTÈME D

Louis XIV and Napoléon were undoubtedly two of the greatest influences on France, and their presence is still felt today in the form of the huge bureaucracy they put in place. The French are ambivalent about this bureaucracy, seeing it simultaneously as the solution to all their problems and the greatest obstacle to solving their problems. The French expect their government to take care of them, to anticipate and meet almost every one of their needs. Yet at the same time they do not have confidence that it will. One in four workers is employed by the state, but those in office jobs often do not think of themselves as public servants but as protected workers who should not have to deal with all the work created by those who need their services. The French know that they are supposed to go to a particular office to get a particular approval even for simple things like getting a phone installed, and that this will probably involve a mountain of paperwork and forms and months of delay. As a result, an alternative way of doing things called Le Système D has evolved. Le Système D, for *débrouillardism*, which, according to Theodore Zeldin in *The French*, means "the art of getting by, of finding one's way through obstacles," is so openly accepted that even the authorities participate in it. John Ardagh and Colin Jones, in *Cultural Atlas of France*, describe a typical situation. "An Englishman with a villa in the Midi wanted electricity installed and was told by the village mayor that it would take years of delay and form-filling. 'But,' he added, 'there's some wiring stacked in the vaults of the [city hall], and René, our electrician, might fix you up, but keep it quiet.'"

costs of raising and educating them. Budget shortfalls as a result of the astronomical cost of trying to meet the French people's expectations of support by their government have made it clear that the French must become less reliant on the state to meet their needs.

A sense of entitlement has also caused a crisis in higher education since the revolts of 1968. Traditionally, any student who passes the *baccalauréat* exam has been entitled to a place at a French university, free of charge. Until the last few decades, interest in continuing formal education beyond high school was fairly low among the middle class, so demand for admission could be easily met. However, beginning

A young woman takes notes during a lecture at the Sorbonne in Paris. An increase in France's student population has led to overcrowding in many of its universities.

in the 1960s, many more women, ethnic minorities, and poorer students have decided to attend. Whereas in 1953 only 7 percent of the age group passed the "*bac*," today 30 percent do. University classrooms are swollen and the number of faculty is insufficient. New universities have been quickly opened, but these are often dreary, overcrowded places in the suburbs, and much of the overcrowding problem is solved by dropouts who simply drift away in dissatisfaction with the experience. How to deal with the growth in student population from 122,000 in 1939 to over a million today, in a way that does not diminish the overall quality of education, has not yet been adequately addressed by the French government, which still maintains strong administrative control of the seventy-seven universities in the system.

POLITICAL CORRUPTION

Other problems facing the French government in recent years have taken a backseat to scandals involving top-rank politicians. The French tolerate (and even expect) some kinds of behavior from political leaders that would be disapproved of in the United States. For example, according to Richard Bernstein, "A mistress is accepted as one of the emblems of success for a man,"[33] rather than a grave moral offense. Likewise, the French are far more relaxed about homosexuality, accepting a politician's sexual orientation without making an issue of it. As to politicians profiting financially from being in office, the French have generally assumed that such profit is one of the privileges of public service. However, in recent years this last situation has changed considerably.

Part of the change is due to a shift in the functions of the courts. Unlike the United States, France does not have a fully independent judiciary. It has state prosecutors (the *parquet*) and examining magistrates called judges, whose role is not

THE CHANGING ROLE OF WOMEN

French women won the right to vote only in 1945, after World War II, and until 1964 a woman had to have her husband's permission to apply for a passport or a bank account. Since that time, such inequities have been made illegal, and in some areas women have made great social and political strides as well. Over a third of the younger generation of doctors are women, and in 1972 the first woman to graduate from the prestigious École Polytechnique showed her competence and suitability by coming in first in the final examinations. Women are now serving as ambassadors and army officers, but they have found breaking into private enterprise at the highest levels more difficult. Business and industry still have few women even in their lower executive levels and almost none at the top of the corporate ladder. In politics, women have occasionally gained top posts. Edith Cresson, for example, became France's first female prime minister in 1991. Part of the problem has been that throughout French history, women have been extraordinarily powerful behind the scenes as mistresses and wives, and as leaders of the influential intellectual and social circles known as salons. For many men and women alike, this arrangement still seems better, and women who wish to be treated equally to men are often seen as odd and confused about their purpose in life.

Edith Cresson became France's first female prime minister in 1991.

to preside over trials but rather to investigate cases before charges are brought. The *parquet* is part of the Ministry of Justice, a division of the government, subject to the directives of whoever is in power. Judges have the latitude to investigate as aggressively as they wish, but only the *parquet* can officially open an investigation. As a result, those in power have known they would be able to stop any inquiries about their own actions from getting very far. However, in the aftermath of the revolts of 1968, some judges and members of the *parquet* began refusing to go along, and newspapers also began printing stories they simply would not have covered before. These various stories implicated top figures, including the mayors of large cities and even a prime minister. According to John Ardagh, "Over 500 political or economic leaders have been convicted, accused, or put under investigation, and in 1993 some 57 parliamentary deputies were facing charges."[34]

The misconduct included bribery and embezzlement of funds, money laundering, and misuse of public funds. The mayor of Cannes was arrested for receiving a suitcase full of banknotes linked to a casino that was underwriting his reelection campaign. Jacques Médecin, mayor of Nice, escaped to Uruguay with only token punishments for embezzlement and other convictions. Even current president Jacques Chirac has faced allegations of corruption dating from his many years as mayor of Paris. Once some of the more shocking and flagrant misconduct was made public, the French faced a new dilemma, which has not been successfully resolved today: Either they could acknowledge that they assumed (and did not care) that their leadership engaged in criminal activities, or they could claim to be more shocked than they were and demand justice that few wanted to see done.

To avoid international scandals that would be embarrassing to the French people as a whole, high-ranking officials accused of corrupt practices are often permitted to make deals to avoid legal proceedings. For example, when Prime Minister Alain Juppé was facing prosecution on charges that he had arranged for his family to live at little cost in luxury apartments owned by the city of Paris, he struck a deal by which his family vacated the premises and no charges were pursued. In a related case, a young judge, Eric Halphen, looked into the finances of Jean Tiberi, a friend of Juppé. A

THE ÉNARQUES

In the past, political power could be achieved in two ways. One could be born into a powerful family, or one could rise through the ranks of local politics. Though these two routes still exist, they have been eclipsed by L'École Nationale d'Admininistration, or the ENA. Founded by Charles de Gaulle in 1945, the ENA was designed to parallel the existing Grandes Écoles (Great Schools), which trained teachers and engineers, but the ENA's mission was different: to train the future leaders of France. It has done this well. President Jacques Chirac is an énarque (as the graduates are known), as is former president Valéry Giscard d'Estaing. In fact, it is now assumed that most top diplomats, legislators, executives, and cabinet members will be énarques. This has had both a positive and negative effect in French politics. Now that leaders of both the Right and Left tend to have been trained together, there is much less political chaos than ever before in French history. On the downside, many criticize the elitism of the ENA, claiming that its graduates are encouraged to have an arrogant and inflated sense of themselves as the anointed future leaders of the country.

Admission to the ENA is coveted. Fewer than two hundred students a year are admitted. The course of study includes training in speaking before television cameras, as well as internships in various ministries. One important feature of ENA training is creative and flexible thinking. Entrance and graduation exams, for example, may consist of only a word, phrase, or short question, drawn from slips of paper in a basket, which the candidate must develop in ninety minutes into an essay and then present as a speech. Recent examples, cited by Richard Bernstein in *Fragile Glory: A Portrait of France and the French*, include "the right man at the right time," "to see," "Can the sciences describe reality?" "regional conflict," "What do you think of the British royal family?" and "the first time." By means of such open-ended topics, students' ability to think and speak quickly with originality and thoughtfulness is developed. Because the French are so fond of debate and quick wit, and because in the information age, "sound bites" often become the only means for politicians to establish their identity and reputation, this training is useful indeed for future leaders.

scandal erupted in the mid-1990s, which made a national celebrity of Halphen, when then Prime Minister Juppé began a campaign against Halphen by harassment of his family, deliberate efforts to move him off the Tiberi case, and the encouragement of insubordination by those assisting Halphen. Halphen and others persisted despite government efforts to stop them, which even went as far as sending a helicopter to the Himalayas to get a vacationing senior judge to overrule a decision by another judge to begin an inquiry into an alleged fraud in which Tiberi's wife and President Chirac have been mentioned as possible defendants.

IMMIGRATION AND RACE

In addition to problems with political corruption, the French today are uncomfortable about other changing aspects of their society. They are caught up in demographic and social changes that are seen by some as enhancing France's vitality and by others as undermining its historical unity and strength. One of the most critical social issues facing France today is immigration because of the growth in racial tensions that has resulted from it. Over the past few decades, France has seen an influx of people from those countries it colonized. In France today, for example, there are approximately 650,000 blacks, most of them from the Caribbean. Because Guadeloupe and Martinique are still considered *départments* of France, islanders who move to France are technically not immigrants but full French citizens. Many Caribbean blacks living in France are well educated and middle class, and though they clearly do not fit the stereotypical physical description of a French man or woman, they nevertheless have had fewer problems making their way in France than some other groups.

One of the groups finding life in France more difficult is the North Africans. Approximately 800,000 Algerians, 550,000 Moroccans, and 220,000 Tunisians are living in France today. Though white emigrants from French overseas colonies faced cultural difficulties repatriating to France, they nevertheless were generally quickly accepted because they were ethnically French. Dark-skinned North Africans have found no such acceptance. Skin color is not the only dividing line, however. Most North Africans are Muslims, and France has had a long-standing inability to accept religious differences

gracefully. Since the 1980s, when unemployment rates began to rise, Muslims have been the target of many of the fears and frustrations of the French people. The extreme right-leaning and openly racist National Front led by Jean-Marie Le Pen continues to use scare tactics to create support for its anti-Muslim and anti-immigrant positions. According to John Ardagh, "Scare stories have been spread of sheep being slaughtered in bathrooms,"[35] and differences between North African Muslim customs and French ones have been blown out of proportion—similar to the way the Protestants were treated as dangerous aliens by the Catholics centuries before.

Complicating the racial tensions surrounding the North African presence in France, which is concentrated in the south and in Paris, are activities by Muslim fundamentalists who commit acts of terrorism and fan hostilities between Muslim immigrants and ethnic French. But typical Muslims, who live primarily in high-rise ghettos on the outskirts of cities, "shunned and despised"[36] by the French, simply want

A group of immigrant children wait for a street concert to begin in their Paris neighborhood.

ANTI-SEMITISM IN FRANCE TODAY

France has a terrible record of anti-Semitism in its history, including the Dreyfus affair at the beginning of the twentieth century. Its worst moment, however, was its complicity in the rounding up and transport of Jews to death camps during World War II. According to scholars John Ardagh and Colin Jones in *Cultural Atlas of France*, "This has left a sense of remorse, and in the main anti-Semitism has now died down" in France today. Still, it is far from dead. National Front members, including their leader Jean-Marie Le Pen, condone and even encourage hatred of Jews, and occasionally neo-Nazi groups desecrate Jewish cemeteries and houses of worship. But typical French people, even those who harbor some anti-Semitic ideas, want nothing to do with violence or harassment of Jews. When Arab terrorists attack kosher restaurants and stores or do damage to synagogues, the response is immediate and strong. Public rallies quickly follow such occurrences, with large and loud crowds proclaiming their views that such outrages must never occur in France again. Nevertheless, many Jews (and others) still view the French culture as deeply anti-Semitic, and the seven hundred thousand Jews living in France—the largest Jewish population in Europe—have not forgotten how quickly their neighbors and fellow citizens have turned against them in the past.

to make a success of life in France. Though the French government has tried to bribe North Africans to return to their land of origin, life is still better for them in France than at home, and as more and more of their children are born in France, the fact seems clear that North Africans are in France to stay. One hopeful sign, according to John Ardagh, is that "many young French people have been shocked by their elders' racism,"[37] and national campaigns against racism have wide support among the younger generations in particular.

Clearly France faces a number of serious problems today, including the fact that in a country that seems sometimes to have an excess of self-pride, only one-third of today's youth report that they are "very proud" to be French.[38] But most would argue that such a mix of self-criticism and self-love is nothing new. France has always been a country where even heated political arguments are seen as no more than interesting and necessary exchanges of viewpoint. It is a country that appears finally to be ready to address the role that its own intolerance and pride have played in eroding its standing in the world community. If somewhat slow to recognize the nation's shortcomings, and often even slower to change, in the new era of globalization and European unity, the French know they must let go of some of the love of being "l'exception française" in favor of remaining a major player on the world stage. But a good loaf of bread and a glass of wine can be enough to begin to dispel the gloom. They are, after all, in France.

FACTS ABOUT FRANCE

GENERAL INFORMATION

Country name: Republic of France

Capital: Paris

Type of government: Republic

Administrative divisions: twenty-two regions; ninety-six *departements;* four overseas *departements* (French Guiana, Guadeloupe, Martinique, Réunion); three overseas territorial collectives (Mayotte, Saint Pierre, and Miquelon); approximately one dozen dependent areas (e.g., French Polynesia)

National holiday: July 14 (Bastille Day, commemorating the start of the French Revolution)

Constitution: September 28, 1958 (commencing the Fifth Republic)

Voting age: Eighteen

Flag: Three equal vertical bands of blue, white, and red, known as the Tricouleur, or Tricolor

GOVERNMENT

Executive Branch

Chief of state: Jacques Chirac (elected May 17, 1995)

Head of government: Prime Minister Lionel Jospin (since June 3, 1997)

Cabinet: Council of Ministers recommended by the prime minister and appointed by the president

Elections: President elected by popular vote for a seven-year term. Next election 2002

Legislative Branch

Two-house Parlement (Parliament) consisting of 321-seat Senate (nine-year terms of office) and 577-seat National Assembly (five-year terms of office)

Judicial Branch

Cour de Cassation (Supreme Court of Appeals): Justices recommended by judiciary committee, appointed by the president

Conseil Constitutionnel (Constitutional Council): Nine members, three appointed by the president, three by each house of Parlement

GEOGRAPHY

Land area: 545,630 square kilometers (341,018 square miles) (excludes overseas holdings); largest Western European nation

Border countries: Andorra, Belgium, Germany, Italy, Luxembourg, Monaco, Spain, and Switzerland

Terrain: mostly plains or gently rolling hills; mountainous in southwest, east

Climate: generally cool winters, mild summers; along the Mediterranean coast, mild winters, hot summers

Natural resources: coal, iron ore, bauxite, fish, timber, zinc, and potash

Land use: 33 percent arable (farmable) land; 22 percent permanent crops and pasturelands; 27 percent forests and woodlands; 18 percent other

Environmental issues: forest damage from acid rain, air pollution from industry and automobiles, water pollution from urban waste and agricultural runoff

PEOPLE

Population: 59,329,691 (mid-2000 estimate)

Age structure: 0–14 years, 19 percent; 15–64 years, 56 percent; 65 and over, 16 percent

Population growth: 0.38 percent

Birthrate: 12.27 births per 1,000 population

Death rate: 9.14 deaths per 1,000 population

Net migration: 0.66 migrants per 1,000 population

Infant mortality rate: 4.51 deaths per 1,000 live births

Life expectancy at birth: 78.76 years

Total fertility rate: 1.75 children born per woman

Religions: Catholic, 90 percent; Protestant, 2 percent; Jewish, 1 percent; Muslim, 1 percent; unaffiliated, 6 percent

ECONOMY

Gross domestic product real growth rate (measure of strength of overall economy): 2.7 percent (1999)

Per capita income: $23,300

Gross domestic product by sector: agriculture, 3.3 percent; industry, 26.1 percent; services, 70.6 percent

Inflation rate: 0.5 percent

Unemployment rate: 11 percent

Budget: revenues, $325 billion; expenditures, $360,000 billion

Industries: steel, machinery, chemicals, automobiles, metallurgy, aircraft, electronics, mining, textiles, food processing, tourism

Electricity production by source: fossil fuel, 10.77 percent; hydro, 12.45 percent; nuclear, 76.24 percent; other, 0.54 percent

Agricultural products: wheat, cereals, sugar beets, potatoes, wine grapes, beef, dairy products, fish

Exports: $304.7 billion (machinery and transportation equipment, chemicals, iron and steel products, agricultural products, textiles and clothing)

Imports: $280.8 billion (crude oil, machinery and equipment, chemi-
cals, agricultural products)

Currency: 1 French franc (F) = 100 centimes

COMMUNICATIONS AND TRANSPORTATION

Telephones: 34.86 million main lines; 11.078 million mobile cellular

Railways: 31,939 kilometers (19,962 miles)

Highways: 893,330 kilometers (558,331 miles)

Waterways: 14,932 kilometers (9,333 miles)

Airports with paved runways: 267

MILITARY

Branches: army, navy, air force, national gendarmerie (national police)

Military registration age: eighteen

Military budget: $39.831 billion (2.5 percent of annual budget)

GLOSSARY

absolutism: Political system in which all power is centered on the monarch.

Anti-Semitism: Hatred of Jews.

arrondissement: Administrative district in Paris.

Blitzkrieg: German term for a style of warfare characterized by sudden, massive assaults by air and land.

colonialism: Movement by countries to establish territory outside their region for military or commercial purposes.

feudalism: Medieval social and economic system of loyalty and bondage of one social group to another, from the king to the serfs in the fields.

Gallic: Adjective derived from Gaul, the Roman word for France, used to describe anything typically French.

Gallo-Roman: Adjective describing the times, achievements, and heritage of the period of Roman influence in Gaul.

guillotine: An execution device consisting of a large mounted blade dropped onto the neck of the victim, severing his or her head.

heresy: A religious belief contrary to the established beliefs of a faith.

hexagon: A six-sided figure.

mass: The Roman Catholic Communion service.

nobility: The class of people born with titles, and usually with hereditary lands.

obelisk: A long, narrow, pointed tower generally used as a monument.

philosophes: Term used for the French thinkers and writers of the eighteenth-century Enlightenment.

rampart: The outer walls of a fortified city.

The Résistance: A term used for the various efforts undertaken by individuals and groups against the Nazi occupiers of France during World War II.

serf: A person legally bound to live and work on a noble's land.

NOTES

INTRODUCTION: THE MANY SIDES OF FRANCE

1. Richard Bernstein, *Fragile Glory: A Portrait of France and the French.* New York: Plume, 1990, p. 36.

CHAPTER 1: LAND OF ABUNDANCE

2. Quoted in *France.* Watford, England: Michelin, 1998, p. 12.

3. *Brittany.* Clermont-Ferrand, France: Michelin, 1983, p. 8.

CHAPTER 2: FROM CAVES TO CATHEDRALS: PREHISTORIC FRANCE THROUGH THE MIDDLE AGES

4. Quoted in Anne Roston, ed., *Insight Guide: France.* Singapore: APA Press, 1989, p. 23.

5. Robert Cole, *A Traveler's History of France.* New York: Interlink Books, 1989, p. 7.

6. Colin Jones, *Cambridge Illustrated History: France.* Cambridge, England: Cambridge University Press, 1994, p. 31.

7. John Ardagh and Colin Jones, *Cultural Atlas of France.* New York: Facts On File, 1991, p. 24.

8. Ardagh and Jones, *Cultural Atlas of France*, p. 30.

9. Ardagh and Jones, *Cultural Atlas of France*, p. 34.

10. Ardagh and Jones, *Cultural Atlas of France*, p. 34.

CHAPTER 3: TORN AND REBORN: THE EARLY MODERN ERA

11. Quoted in Jones, *France.* p. 119.

12. Quoted in Jones, *France*, p. 140.

13. Jones, *France*, p. 164.

14. Fiona Duncan, ed., *Insight Guide: France.* New York: Langenscheidt, 1999, p. 37.

15. Jones, *France*, p. 175.

16. Ardagh and Jones, *Cultural Atlas of France*, p. 59.

17. Cole, *Traveler's History*, p. 115.

CHAPTER 4: FRANCE IN THE MODERN ERA

18. Jones, *France*, p. 217.

19. Duncan, *France*, p. 44.

20. Quoted in Jones, *France*, p. 220.

21. Quoted in Ardagh and Jones, *Cultural Atlas of France*, p. 89.

22. Ardagh and Jones, *Cultural Atlas of France*, p. 90.

23. Jones, *France*, p. 282.

24. Quoted in Jones, *France*, p. 309.

25. Duncan, *France*, p. 58.

CHAPTER 5: WORK, LEISURE, AND FAMILY LIFE

26. Theodore Zeldin, *The French*. New York: Kodansha International, 1996, p. 207.

27. Sally Adamson Taylor, *Culture Shock: France*. Portland, OR: Graphic Arts Publishing, 1996, p. 153.

28. Ardagh and Jones, *Cultural Atlas of France*, p. 128.

29. Ardagh and Jones, *Cultural Atlas of France*, p. 127.

CHAPTER 6: SUBTLETY AND SURPRISE: ARTS AND CULTURE IN FRANCE

30. Ardagh and Jones, *Cultural Atlas of France*, p. 144.

31. Louis-Bernard Robitaille, *And God Created the French*. Montreal: Robert Davies Press, 1995, p. 196.

CHAPTER 7: CONTEMPORARY FRANCE: CHALLENGES AND CHANGES

32. John Ardagh, *France in the New Century: Portrait of a Changing Society*. London: Penguin Books, 2000, p. 11.

33. Bernstein, *Fragile Glory*, p. 171.

34. Ardagh, *France in the New Century*, p. 41.

35. Ardagh and Jones, *Cultural Atlas of France*, p. 116.

36. Ardagh and Jones, *Cultural Atlas of France*, p. 116.

37. Ardagh and Jones, *Cultural Atlas of France*, pp. 116–17.

38. Ardagh and Jones, *Cultural Atlas of France*, p. 113.

CHRONOLOGY

18,000 B.C.

Cave drawings created at Lascaux, Cosquer, and elsewhere in France.

5000 B.C.

Menhirs, dolmens, and other rock structures created.

1000 B.C.

Celts arrive in France.

52 B.C.

Vercingetorix defeated by the Romans, bringing Gallo-Roman Wars to an end.

476

Overthrow of last Roman emperor brings Roman occupation of Gaul to an end.

481–511

Rule of Clovis, first king of France.

732

Battle of Poitiers stops expansion of Islam in Europe.

800

Charlemagne crowned holy Roman emperor.

987

Capetian dynasty founded by Hugh Capet.

1095

First Crusade launched.

1208

Pope Innocent III declares crusade against the Cathars.

1245

Last Cathar stronghold at Montségur captured; two hundred Cathars burned alive.

1337

Hundred Years' War with England starts.

1348

Black Death arrives in France.

1429

Joan of Arc leads French troops at Orléans; dauphin is crowned at Reims.

1431

Joan of Arc burned at stake at Rouen.

1453

End of Hundred Years' War.

1562–1598

Wars of religion.

1572

St. Bartholomew's Eve Massacre.

1598

Edict of Nantes establishes religious tolerance as state policy.

1643–1715

Reign of Louis XIV, the Sun King.

1789

Storming of the Bastille starts the French Revolution.

1793

Execution of Louis XVI and his family.

1794

Robespierre is executed, marking end of Reign of Terror.

1804

Napoléon crowned emperor.

1815

Napoléon returns from exile on Elba; defeated at Waterloo.

1830

Louis Philippe's July Monarchy begins.

1848

Louis Philippe deposed; Second Republic declared.

1851

Louis Napoléon declares himself emperor.

1871

Paris Commune uprising ends with mass murder by police.

1889

Universal Exhibition of Paris; construction of Eiffel Tower.

1897–1899

Dreyfus affair reveals corruption and anti-Semitism in
French army.

1914–1918

World War I.

1939–1945

World War II.

1940

Paris occupied by Germans; Marshal Henri Pétain
establishes Vichy government; Charles de Gaulle calls
for resistance.

1944

Allied landing in Normandy leads to liberation of France.

1954

France withdraws from Indochina; Algerian insurrection
begins.

1959

General de Gaulle elected president.

1962

Algerian independence.

1968

Student protests lead to national revolts.

1969

De Gaulle resigns presidency; Georges Pompidou elected president.

1974

Valéry Giscard d'Estaing elected president.

1981

François Mitterand elected president.

1986

Jacques Chirac becomes prime minister.

1989

Bicentennial celebration of French Revolution; Louvre Pyramid, Grande Arche, and Opera Bastille officially dedicated.

1995

Jacques Chirac elected president.

1997

Socialist Lionel Jospin becomes prime minister.

1998

National elections reveal growing strength of extremist National Front.

SUGGESTIONS FOR FURTHER READING

Stephen E. Ambrose, *D-Day: June 6, 1944: The Climactic Battle of World War II.* New York: Simon & Schuster, 1994. Written by a noted expert and director of an oral D-Day archive in New Orleans, this book was published to commemorate the fiftieth anniversary of the Normandy invasion.

Veronique Bussolin, *France.* Austin, TX: Raintree Steck-Vaughan, 1995. One in a series of Country Fact Files for young adult readers, this book provides an overview of important statistics and other facts about France.

Francoise Cachin, *Gauguin: The Quest for Paradise.* New York: Harry N. Abrams Press, 1992. This volume in the Discoveries series for young adult readers gives a strong introduction to the life and works of Paul Gauguin. Other volumes focus on other French artists, including Picasso and Degas.

Gilles Desmons, *Walking Paris: Thirty Original Walks In and Around Paris.* New York: McGraw-Hill, 1999. The author takes readers to out-of-the-way places with writing lively and clear enough to allow readers to get a good impression of what Paris is really like.

Allen French, *The Red Keep: A Story of Burgundy in 1165.* Warsaw, ND: Bethlehem Books, August 1997. Acclaimed book in the Adventure Library series for young adult readers by a Harvard historian whose goal is to present information about historical periods and systems of government within the context of an exciting adventure story. Illustrated by prominent artist Andrew Wyeth.

Ethel Caro Gofen, *France.* New York: Marshall Cavendish, 1992. One book in the Cultures of the World series, this book for young adults provides basic information about France.

Jonathan Harris, *The Land and the People of France.* New York: HarperCollins, 1989. Good basic text for young adults, but somewhat dated and lacking in illustrations and photos.

Susan Herrmann Loomis, *On Rue Tatin.* New York: Broadway Books, 2001. Details the author's early experiences attending cooking school in France and her subsequent life in a converted French monastery, centering on recipes and cooking anecdotes.

Peter Mayle, *A Year in Provence.* New York: Vintage Books, 1991. Best-selling story of the author's early experiences living in rural France. Mayle followed up with *Toujours Provence*, also a lively read.

Stephen O'Shea, *The Perfect Heresy: The Revolutionary Life and Death of the Medieval Cathars.* New York: Walker, 2000. Journalist and translator Stephen O'Shea brings facts about the Cathars and their beliefs to life in a clearly written book.

Cornelius Ryan, *The Longest Day: June 6, 1944.* New York: Touchstone Books, 1994. A classic historical narrative of the D-Day invasion, originally written in the 1950s and made into a movie of the same name, Ryan's book was recently reprinted.

James Startt, *Tour de France/Tour de Force: A Visual History of the World's Greatest Bicycle Race.* San Francisco: Chronicle Books, 2000. Well-illustrated history of the race and profiles of famous riders, including Greg Lemond, who wrote the introduction.

Ann Waldron, *Claude Monet.* New York: Harry N. Abrams Press, 1991. One in a series of books in the First Impressions series on French Impressionist painters.

Jude Welton, *Eyewitness Art: Impressionism.* New York: DK Publishing, 1993. This volume, one in a series on different artistic periods, is a well-organized and visually presented work focusing on interesting facts about the artists' techniques as well as their lives and works.

WEBSITES

France.com. (www.france.com): Links to news and cultural information are highlights of this thorough and well-structured site.

FranceWay. (www.franceway.com): Good site primarily for those planning trips, but with good general information as well.

French Embassy in the United States. (www.info-france-usa. org). Excellent and well organized official site, with a special section for young people, providing information of interest to them about events, life, and culture in France.

Lonely Planet World Guide: France. (www.lonelyplanet.com): A condensed version of the print version of this famous guide.

Les Pages de Paris/Paris Pages. (www.paris.org): Very entertaining site containing extensive information about all aspects of Paris and Parisian life.

WORKS CONSULTED

Matthew Alice, "Straight from the Hip," *San Diego Reader*, August 16, 2001, p. 12. This regular column in the *San Diego Reader* answers a reader's question about the effect of accents on French advertising.

John Ardagh, *France in the New Century: Portrait of a Changing Society*. London: Penguin Books, 2000. Thorough discussion of all aspects of contemporary France by a noted British journalist.

John Ardagh and Colin Jones, *Cultural Atlas of France*. New York: Facts On File, 1991. Outstanding volume, well illustrated with maps, photographs, and illustrations, including strong text on history, culture, and current events, and informative sidebars on specific subjects of interest to readers.

Richard Bernstein, *Fragile Glory: A Portrait of France and the French*. New York: Plume, 1990. Excellent and insightful work by a *New York Times* correspondent stationed in Paris.

Brittany. Clermont-Ferrand, France: Michelin, 1983. One in a series of guidebooks about France.

Robert Cole, *A Traveler's History of France*. New York: Interlink Books, 1989. One in a series of Traveler's Guides, this brief history is by an eminent American historian.

Fiona Duncan, ed., *Insight Guide: France*. New York: Langenscheidt, 1999. This volume in the Insight Guide series provides a lavishly photographed introduction to the places and people of France.

France. Watford, England: Michelin, 1998. A volume in what is widely reputed to be the most thorough and authoritative travel guide series in the world.

Joseph and Frances Gies, *Life in a Medieval City*. New York: HarperPerennial, 1969. This interesting and readable text depicts in detail what it was like to live in the French city of Troyes in the twelfth and thirteenth centuries.

Julian Jackson, *France: The Dark Years, 1940–1944.* Oxford: Oxford University Press, 2001. Upon its recent release, this book by one of today's top scholars was immediately deemed to be the authoritative text on the Nazi occupation of France.

Colin Jones, *Cambridge Illustrated History: France.* Cambridge, England: Cambridge University Press, 1994. Very readable text, full of illustrations, charts and tables, sidebars, and photographs, which bring French history to life.

Roger Price, *A Concise History of France.* Cambridge, England: Cambridge University Press, 1993. Clear and informative history by an eminent professor of French history.

Louis-Bernard Robitaille, *And God Created the French.* Montreal: Robert Davies Press, 1995. An irreverent best-seller about French attitudes and behaviors by a French Canadian journalist who has lived for years in Paris as a correspondent for a Montreal newspaper.

Anne Roston, ed., *Insight Guide: France.* Singapore: APA Press, 1989. Wonderful photos and information about France.

Sally Adamson Taylor, *Culture Shock: France.* Portland, OR: Graphic Arts Publishing, 1996. One in a series of Culture Shock titles, this book details the small customs and differences in views that are essential to an accurate understanding and interpretation of French behavior.

Theodore Zeldin, *The French.* New York: Kodansha International, 1996. Classic work on the French people by a noted historian.

WEBSITE:

The World Factbook 2000: France. (www.cia.gov/cia/ publications/factbook/geos/fr.html). An on-line condensed version of the information contained in the Factbooks published by the Library of Congress, used by diplomats, the military, and others doing business or otherwise interested in statistics and other information about France.

INDEX

123

PICTURE CREDITS

ABOUT THE AUTHOR

Laurel Corona lives in Lake Arrowhead, California, and teaches English and humanities at San Diego City College. She has a master's degree from the University of Chicago and a Ph.D. from the University of California at Davis. Dr. Corona has written many other books for Lucent Books, including *Brazil, Ethiopia, Life in Moscow, Norway,* and *Peru.*